vegetarian

appetizers & snacks • soups & salads • pasta
& grains • veggies & beans • just desserts

mc
rae
PUBLISHING

This book was conceived, edited and designed by
McRae Publishing Ltd
London

www.mcraebooks.com

NOTE TO OUR READERS
Eating eggs or egg whites that are not completely cooked poses the possibility of salmonella food poisoning. The risk is greater for pregnant women, the elderly, the very young, and persons with impaired immune systems. If you are concerned about salmonella, you can use reconstituted powdered egg whites or pasteurized eggs.

Culinary Notebooks series

Project Director Anne McRae
Art Director Marco Nardi

VEGETARIAN
Photography Brent Parker Jones
Text Carla Bardi
Editing Christine Price, Daphne Trotter
Food Styling Lee Blaylock
Food Preparation and Assistant Stylists Mark Hockenhull, Milli Lee
Layouts Aurora Granata

ISBN 978-88-6098-359-6

Printed in China

contents

getting started

Vegetarian food is delicious, and it is also healthy—for ourselves, and for our planet as a whole. Here you will find 100 tempting dishes for every occasion. Almost all the recipes are easy to prepare. To help you choose the right dish, we have rated them for difficulty: 1 (simple), 2 (fairly simple), or 3 (challenging). In these two pages we have highlighted 25 of the most enticing recipes, just to get you started!

● SIMPLE

TAPENADE & GOAT CHEESE toasts

STUFFED eggs

CHILLED AVOCADO
soup

PEARL BARLEY with
sundried tomato pesto

RHUBARB crumble

ROASTED GARLIC
hummus

LENTIL & SWEET POTATO
soup

● HEALTHY

WARM LENTIL & GOAT CHEESE salad

QUINOA SALAD
with celery & almonds

PURPLE FRUIT
salad

VEGETARIAN CLASSICS

VEGETARIAN paella

SAMOSAS

TOMATO soup

EGGPLANT
parmigiana

SPECIAL OCCASION
carrot cake

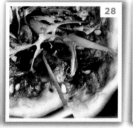

GREEK
pizza

PEARL BARLEY
risotto

EDITOR'S CHOICE

PASTA SALAD with blue cheese & cumin

SPICY TOFU
stir-fry

RASPBERRY
tart

BEST SNACK

BEST SOUP

BEST SALAD

BEST VEGGIE DISH

BEST DESSERT

PARMESAN palmiers

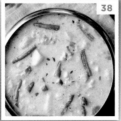

VEGETABLE
chowder

PANZANELLA

BAKED RISOTTO
tomatoes

CHOCOLATE-DIPPED
almond strawberries

snacks & appetizers

TOMATO & GOAT CHEESE tart

1	(8-ounce/250-g) sheet ready-rolled puff pastry
1	tablespoon sour cream
1	teaspoon grainy mustard
	Salt and freshly ground black pepper
2	tablespoons extra-virgin olive oil
2	large leeks, white and light-green parts only, thinly sliced
8-10	cherry tomatoes, quartered
4	ounces (120 g) fresh goat cheese, crumbled
	Fresh basil leaves

Serves 4 • Preparation 15 minutes + 15 minutes to chill • Cooking 20–25 minutes • Difficulty 1

1. Preheat the oven to 400°F (200°C/gas 6). Line a large baking sheet with parchment paper. Unroll the sheet of pastry and place on the baking sheet.

2. Stir the sour cream and mustard in a small bowl. Season with salt and pepper. Spread the sour cream mixture evenly over the pastry. Fold in a $1/2$-inch (1-cm) border on all sides. Chill for 15 minutes.

3. Heat the oil in a large frying pan over medium-low heat. Add the leeks and sauté until very soft, 8–10 minutes. Spread the leek mixture evenly over the sour cream mixture. Top with the cherry tomatoes and season with salt and pepper.

4. Bake for 20–25 minutes, until the pastry is crisp and golden brown. Top with the goat cheese and basil. Serve warm or at room temperature.

If you liked this recipe, you will love these as well.

ONION focaccia

LEMON & PARMESAN pizza

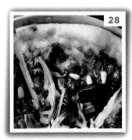

GREEK pizza

ROASTED EGGPLANT dip

1 large eggplant (aubergine), weighing about 1$\frac{1}{2}$ pounds (750 g)

1 cup (250 ml) crème fraîche or sour cream

Freshly squeezed juice of 1 lemon

Salt and freshly ground black pepper

Fresh cilantro (coriander) leaves, to garnish

Toasted pita bread, to serve

Serves 4 • Preparation 15 minutes • Cooking 45–50 minutes
Difficulty 1

1. Preheat the oven to 350°F (180°C/gas 4). Roast the eggplant for 45–50 minutes, until tender. Set aside until cool enough to handle.

2. Peel off and discard the blackened skin. Put the flesh in a food processor and chop until almost smooth. Leave a little bit of texture.

3. Transfer to a serving bowl. Stir in the crème fraîche and lemon juice. Season with salt and pepper. Garnish with the cilantro. Serve warm with the pita bread.

ROASTED GARLIC hummus

6   large cloves garlic, unpeeled

1   tablespoon + 1 teaspoon extra-virgin olive oil

1   (14-ounce/400-g) can garbanzo beans (chickpeas), drained and rinsed

1/4   cup (60 ml) freshly squeezed lemon juice

3   tablespoons sesame tahini

3   tablespoons water

1/2   teaspoon salt

1/4   teaspoon cayenne pepper

1/4   cup fresh chives, finely chopped

Carrot sticks, to serve

Cucumber sticks, to serve

Celery stalks, to serve

Serves 4 • Preparation 15 minutes • Cooking 20 minutes • Difficulty 1

1. Preheat the oven to 400°F (200°C/gas 6). Place the garlic cloves on a small piece of aluminum foil and drizzle with 1 teaspoon of oil. Wrap in the foil and roast for 20 minutes, until softened.

2. Let cool slightly, then peel and transfer to a food processor. Add the garbanzo beans and chop until smooth.

3. Add the lemon juice, tahini, water, salt, cayenne, and remaining oil, and process until creamy. Stir in the chives and transfer to a serving bowl. Serve with the carrots, cucumber, and celery.

Tapenade is a delicious Provençal dish, made by finely chopping green or black olives with capers, anchovies, and olive oil.

TAPENADE & GOAT CHEESE toasts

1	baguette (French loaf), sliced on the diagonal, toasted
2	cups (100 g) pitted black olives
1	ounce (30 g) anchovy fillets
2	cloves garlic
1	tablespoon brine-cured capers, drained
2	tablespoons freshly squeezed lemon juice
5	ounces (150 g) soft fresh goat cheese
3	tablespoons fresh thyme leaves + extra, to garnish
5	tablespoons finely chopped walnuts

Serves 6-8 • Preparation 10 minutes • Cooking 3-5 minutes • Difficulty 1

1. Preheat the oven to 400°F (200°C/gas 6). Spread the bread out on a large baking sheet and toast for 3-5 minutes, turning once, until golden brown. Place on a wire rack and let cool a little.

2. Combine the olives, anchovies, garlic, capers, and lemon juice in a food processor and chop until smooth.

3. Mix the goat cheese, thyme, and walnuts in a bowl and spread over the toasts. Top with the tapenade. Garnish with the extra thyme and serve.

If you liked this recipe, you will love these as well.

ROASTED EGGPLANT
dip

CARAMELIZED ONION
dip

BLUE CHEESE
& WALNUT crostini

CARAMELIZED ONION dip

Serves 6-8 • Preparation 15 minutes + 1 hour to chill • Cooking 12-15 minutes • Difficulty 1

1	tablespoon extra-virgin olive oil	1½	teaspoons white wine vinegar
1	pound (500 g) white onions, finely chopped	½	cup finely chopped fresh cilantro (coriander)
	Salt and freshly ground black pepper		Crackers, to serve
1	cup (250 ml) sour cream		Carrot sticks, to serve
2	ounces (60 g) cream cheese, softened		

1. Heat the oil in a large frying pan over medium heat. Add the onions, season with salt and pepper, and simmer, stirring frequently, until golden brown, 12-15 minutes. Let cool to room temperature.

2. Combine the onions, sour cream, cream cheese, vinegar, and cilantro in a bowl. Season with salt and pepper.

3. Chill until slightly thickened, about 1 hour. Serve with the crackers and carrots.

TWO-IN-ONE dip

Serves 4-6 • Preparation 15 minutes • Difficulty 1

1	(14-ounce/400-g) can garbanzo beans (chickpeas), drained and rinsed	4	tablespoons (60 ml) extra-virgin olive oil
3	cups (150 g) fresh cilantro (coriander) leaves	2	teaspoons freshly squeezed lemon juice
2	cloves garlic, chopped	2-4	tablespoons cold water
1	ripe avocado, pitted and coarsely chopped		Salt and freshly ground black pepper
			Tortilla chips, to serve
			Carrot sticks, to serve
			Celery stalks, to serve

1. Combine the garbanzo beans, cilantro, garlic, and avocado in a food processor and whizz until finely chopped.

2. Add the oil in a slow, steady trickle. Add the lemon juice and then the water, 1 tablespoon at a time, until the mixture is smooth. Season with salt and pepper.

3. Serve with the tortilla chips, carrot sticks, and celery.

ZUCCHINI fritters

Serves 6-8 • Preparation 20 minutes + 1 hour to chill • Cooking 15-20 minutes • Difficulty 2

4	large zucchini (courgettes)	2	tablespoons finely chopped fresh parsley
1	cup (125 g) freshly grated Parmesan cheese	2	tablespoons finely chopped fresh mint
2	large eggs		Salt and freshly ground black pepper
1-2	cups (150-300 g) fine dry bread crumbs	1	cup (250 ml) olive oil, for frying

1. Cook the zucchini in salted, boiling water until almost tender, about 5 minutes. Drain and let cool slightly. Pat dry, then chop finely with a knife.

2. Transfer to a large bowl and mix in the cheese, eggs, parsley, mint, salt, and pepper, and enough bread crumbs to make a firm mixture.

3. Dust your hands with flour and shape the mixture into balls about the size of walnuts. Roll in the remaining bread crumbs. Chill for 1 hour.

4. Heat the oil in a large frying pan. Fry the fritters in batches until golden and crisp, 5-7 minutes each batch. Drain on paper towels. Serve hot.

STUFFED eggs

Serves 4-8 • Preparation 20 minutes • Cooking 7 minutes Difficulty 1

8	large eggs	1	clove garlic, finely chopped
⅓	cup (90 ml) mayonnaise	2	teaspoons finely chopped fresh cilantro
1	tablespoon Dijon mustard		Salt and freshly ground black pepper
1	teaspoon white wine vinegar		Paprika, to dust

1. Place the eggs in a medium saucepan and add enough cold water to cover. Bring to a boil, then simmer for 7 minutes. Drain and run the eggs under cold water to cool.

2. Combine the mayonnaise, mustard, vinegar, garlic, and cilantro in a small bowl.

3. Peel the eggs, and halve lengthwise. Use a small teaspoon to remove the yolks, leaving the whites intact. Add the yolks to the bowl with the mayonnaise mixture and season with salt and pepper. Mash with a fork until smooth.

4. Spoon the yolk mixture into the whites. Dust with paprika, and serve.

BLUE CHEESE & WALNUT crostini

4   ounces (120 g) cream cheese
$\frac{1}{2}$ cup (60 g) walnuts, chopped
      Freshly ground black pepper
4   ounces (120 g) blue cheese, such as Gorgonzola or Stilton
1   baguette (French loaf), slice on the diagonal
1   tablespoon coarsely chopped fresh parsley, to garnish

Serves 4 • Preparation 15 minutes • Cooking 8–15 minutes • Difficulty 1

1. Preheat the oven to 400°F (200°C/gas 6). Spread the bread out on a large baking sheet and toast for 3–5 minutes, turning once, until golden brown. Place on a wire rack and let cool a little.

2. Stir the cream cheese and walnuts in a bowl until smooth. Season with pepper. Stir in the blue cheese.

3. Spread the mixture evenly on the toast and bake for 5–10 minutes, until melted and bubbling. Sprinkle with the parsley and serve warm.

SPINACH & PHYLLO slice

2 tablespoons extra-virgin olive oil + extra, to brush
1 onion, finely chopped
4 cloves garlic, finely chopped
2½ pounds (1.25 kg) baby spinach
5 ounces (150 g) feta cheese, crumbled
¼ cup (30 g) golden raisins (sultanas), chopped
   Salt and freshly ground black pepper
20 sheets phyllo (filo) pastry, cut into 8 x 12-inch (20 x 30-cm) rectangles

Serves 8–12 • Preparation 30 minutes • Cooking 50–60 minutes
Difficulty 2

1. Preheat the oven to 350°F (180°C/gas 4). Line a large baking sheet with parchment paper. Heat the oil in a large frying pan over medium heat. Add the onion and garlic and sauté until golden, 3–4 minutes. Transfer to a large bowl.

2. Return the pan to the heat. Cook the spinach in batches, tossing until wilted, 1–2 minutes each batch. Chop coarsely. Add the spinach, feta, and raisins to the bowl. Season with salt and pepper.

3. Place a sheet of phyllo on a work surface and brush with oil. Lay another sheet on top and brush with oil. Repeat until you have 10 layers. Spread half the filling lengthwise down the center. Roll into a log and brush with oil. Make eight small cuts across the top. Repeat with remaining phyllo and filling.

4. Place the logs, seam-side down, on the prepared baking sheet. Bake for 45–50 minutes, until golden brown. Slice and serve warm or at room temperature.

These wraps make a healthy after-school snack or weekend lunch. For a change in flavor, replace the guacamole with one of the dips featured in the boxes at the bottom of the page.

GRILLED VEGGIE WRAPS with guacamole

Salsa

6	ripe tomatoes, diced
1	clove garlic, finely chopped
1	small onion, finely chopped
1/2	fresh green chili, seeded and finely chopped
1	tablespoon finely chopped fresh cilantro (coriander)

Guacamole

2	ripe avocados, peeled and stoned
2	tablespoons freshly squeezed lime juice
1	clove garlic, finely chopped
1	small onion, finely chopped
3	small tomatoes, chopped
1/4	fresh green chili, seeded and finely chopped
1	tablespoon finely chopped fresh cilantro (coriander)

Wraps

1	zucchini (courgette), cut into long thin slices lengthwise
1	red bell pepper (capsicum), seeded and cut into long strips lengthwise
1	yellow bell pepper (capsicum), seeded and cut into long strips lengthwise
4	large flour tortillas

Serves 4 • Preparation 30 minutes + 30 minutes to stand • Cooking 20–25 minutes • Difficulty 1

Salsa

1. Mix the tomatoes, garlic, onion, chili, and cilantro in a bowl. Let stand for 30 minutes at room temperature.

Guacamole

1. Mash the avocados with the lime juice, garlic, onion, tomato, chili, and cilantro in a bowl until almost smooth.

Wraps

1. Heat a grill pan over medium-high heat. Add the zucchini and bell peppers and grill until softened and marked with black lines.

2. Heat the tortillas in the grill pan. Spread with one tablespoon each of guacamole and salsa.

3. Divide the vegetables evenly among the four tortillas. Wrap up and return to the grill pan for one minute on each side. Serve warm with the extra salsa and guacamole.

If you liked this recipe, you will love these as well.

ROASTED GARLIC hummus

CARAMELIZED ONION dip

TWO-IN-ONE dip

PARMESAN palmiers

1   (8-ounce/250-g) sheet ready rolled puff pastry

1   tablespoon extra-virgin olive oil

$1/3$ cup (40 g) freshly grated Parmesan cheese

3   tablespoons freshly grated Emmenthal cheese

1   tablespoon finely chopped fresh thyme

      Freshly ground black pepper

1   large egg yolk

$1/2$ teaspoon water

Serves 6–8 • Preparation 15 minutes + 15 minutes to chill • Cooking 15–20 minutes • Difficulty 1

1. Preheat the oven to 375°F (190°C/gas 5). Line two large baking sheets with parchment paper. Unroll the pastry on a lightly floured work surface. Brush with the oil and sprinkle with the cheeses, thyme, and pepper.

2. Fold the longest sides of the pastry inward by 1 inch (2.5 cm), then roll the long sides inward until they meet in the center. Chill for 15 minutes. Cut into $1/4$-inch (5-mm) slices. Place on the prepared baking sheets, spacing 1 inch (2.5 cm) apart.

3. Whisk the egg yolk and water in a bowl. Brush over the palmiers. Bake for 15–20 minutes, until golden brown. Let cool for 2 minutes on the baking sheets, then transfer to wire racks and let cool. Serve warm or at room temperature.

CHEESE straws

1 (12-ounce/350-g) sheet ready rolled puff pastry
1 large egg, lightly beaten
1 cup (120 g) freshly grated Parmesan cheese
White sesame seeds

Serves 8–12 • Preparation 20 minutes + 30 minutes to chill • Cooking 15 minutes • Difficulty 1

1. Unroll the pastry on a lightly floured work surface. Brush with some of the beaten egg. Sprinkle the bottom half of the dough with half the cheese. Fold the top half over the cheese, pressing down gently all over.

2. Roll out the dough into an 8 x 12-inch (20 x 30-cm) rectangle. Brush with more beaten egg. Sprinkle evenly with the remaining cheese, pressing down gently all over. Trim the edges to form a neat rectangle.

3. Cut the dough into $1/4$-inch (5-m) strips. Twist into spirals. Sprinkle half the cheese straws with the sesame seeds. Place on baking sheets, spacing about $1/2$ inch (1 cm) apart. Cover with plastic wrap (cling film) and chill 30 minutes.

4. Preheat the oven to 375°F (190°C/gas 5). Bake for 15 minutes, until golden brown. Transfer to a wire rack to cool. Serve warm or at room temperature.

These tasty little treats make a great addition to a buffet or party spread. Prepare them ahead of time, then pop them into the oven about half an hour before you intend to serve them.

CHEESE & VEGGIE pasties

Filling
1 yellow bell pepper (capsicum), seeds removed, cut into small pieces
3 carrots, cut into small cubes
12 ounces (350 g) butternut squash, peeled, seeds removed, cut into small cubes
1 (2-inch/5-cm) piece fresh ginger, grated
1/2 teaspoon ground cumin
4 tablespoons finely chopped fresh cilantro (coriander)
4 scallions (spring onions), trimmed and finely chopped
1 (7-ounce/200-g) can corn (sweetcorn) kernels, drained and rinsed
1 cup (120 g) freshly grated Cheddar or Gruyere cheese
Freshly ground black pepper

Pastry
1 1/2 cups (225 g) all-purpose (plain) flour
1 teaspoon ground turmeric
1/4 teaspoon salt
1/2 cup (120 g) cold unsalted butter, cut into small cubes
4-5 tablespoons (60-75 ml) iced water
1 large egg, lightly beaten

Serves 6-12 • Preparation 45 minutes + 30 minutes to chill • Cooking 20-25 minutes • Difficulty 2

Filling
1. Put the bell pepper, carrots, and squash in a saucepan and pour in enough boiling water to cover. Bring to a boil, then simmer until tender, 4-5 minutes. Drain well.
2. Transfer the drained vegetables to a large bowl and add all the remaining filling ingredients. Mix until well combined, then set aside until completely cool.
3. Preheat the oven to 400°F (200°C/gas 6). Line a large baking sheet with parchment paper.

Pastry
1. Sift the flour, turmeric, and salt in a bowl. Rub in the butter with your fingertips until the mixture resembles fine bread crumbs. Add the water, 1 tablespoon at a time, stirring until the dough comes together. Roll into a ball, wrap in plastic wrap (cling film), and chill for 30 minutes.
2. Roll out the pastry on a lightly floured work surface to 1/4 inch (5 mm) thick. Cut out twelve 2-inch (5-cm) disks from the pastry using a cookie cutter or glass.
3. Divide the filling mixture evenly among the pastry disks, covering only one half of each disk and leaving a small border around the edge. Brush the edges of the pastry lightly with beaten egg. Fold the free half of each disk over the filling, pressing down on the edges with a fork to seal. Brush with the remaining beaten egg.
4. Arrange on the prepared baking sheet. Bake for 20-25 minutes, until golden brown. Serve warm.

FALAFEL

1   (14-ounce/400-g) can garbanzo beans (chickpeas), drained and rinsed
2   cloves garlic, chopped
1   small onion, chopped
4   tablespoons chopped fresh parsley
2   tablespoons chopped fresh mint
1/2   teaspoon ground cumin
1/2   teaspoon ground coriander
1/4   teaspoon cayenne pepper
1/4   teaspoon baking soda (bicarbonate of soda)
3/4   teaspoon salt
2   tablespoons freshly squeezed lemon juice
1   large egg, lightly beaten
3   tablespoons sesame seeds, toasted
1/2   cup (120 ml) canola oil

Serves 4–6 • Preparation 15 minutes + 30 minutes to chill • Cooking 10–15 minutes • Difficulty 2

1. Place half the garbanzo beans in a food processor and pulse until coarsely chopped. Transfer to a large bowl.

2. Put the remaining garbanzo beans in the food processor with the garlic, onion, parsley, mint, cumin, coriander, cayenne, baking soda, salt, and lemon juice. Chop to a thick, chunky paste. Add to the bowl with the coarsely chopped garbanzos. Stir in the egg and sesame seeds. Cover the bowl and chill for 30 minutes.

3. Heat the oil in a large frying pan over medium heat. Cook the falafel in batches by dropping heaped spoonfuls of batter into the pan. Fry, turning once, until deep golden brown on both sides, 4–5 minutes. Drain on paper towels. Serve hot.

HALLOUMI, ZUCCHINI & TOMATO skewers

1 teaspoon chile powder

1/2 cup coarsely chopped fresh basil

3 tablespoons freshly squeezed lemon juice

2 teaspoons finely grated unwaxed lemon zest

1/2 cup (120 ml) extra-virgin olive oil

2 zucchini (courgettes), sliced into rounds

16 grape or small cherry tomatoes

8 ounces (250 g) halloumi cheese, cubed

Serves 4–6 • Preparation 15 minutes + 30 minutes to marinate
Cooking 8–10 minutes • Difficulty 1

1. Whisk the chile powder, basil, lemon juice, lemon zest, and oil in a small bowl. Put the zucchini, tomatoes, and halloumi in a large shallow dish and drizzle with the oil mixture. Stir well to coat. Set aside to marinate for 30 minutes. Soak 12 wooden skewers for 30 minutes.

2. Preheat an overhead broiler (grill), indoor grill, or barbecue on medium-high.

3. Thread the zucchini, tomatoes, and halloumi onto the skewers. Broil (grill) until the cheese is hot and the vegetables are softening, 8–10 minutes. Turn and baste with the marinade during cooking. Serve hot.

23

Samosas are a favorite snack food all over the Indian subcontinent, and in many parts of Central and Southeast Asia, the Middle East, and Africa. Serve them hot, straight from the pan.

SAMOSAS

Pastry

$1^1/_3$	cups (200 g) all-purpose (plain) flour
$^1/_2$	teaspoon baking powder
$^1/_8$	teaspoon salt
1	tablespoon ghee (clarified butter)
3	tablespoons warm milk + more, as needed

Filling

1	potato, peeled and diced
1	small onion, finely chopped
1	tomato, chopped
2	tablespoons ghee (clarified butter)
1	tablespoon garam masala
1	teaspoon ground coriander
1	teaspoon grated fresh ginger
$^1/_2$	teaspoon chile powder
$^2/_3$	cup (100 g) frozen peas
1	tablespoon freshly squeezed lemon juice
2	cups (500 ml) peanut oil, for frying

Serves 4–6 • Preparation 30 minutes • Cooking 30–40 minutes
Difficulty 2

Pastry

1. Sift the flour, baking powder, and salt into a bowl. Mix in the ghee and enough of the milk to form a stiff dough. Turn the dough out onto a lightly floured surface and knead until smooth.

2. Roll out into a large rectangle and cut into 12 strips measuring about 3 x 8 inches (8 x 20 cm).

Filling

1. Cook the potato in a large pot of salted boiling water until tender, 8–10 minutes. Drain and set aside.

2. Sauté the onion and tomato in the ghee in a frying pan over medium heat until softened, 3–4 minutes. Mix in the garam masala, coriander, ginger, chile powder, peas, and potato, and cook for 5 minutes. Drizzle with the lemon juice.

3. Place a tablespoon of the filling in the center of each pastry strip. Brush the edges with water and fold over to form a triangle. Press down on the edges to seal.

4. Heat the oil in a large, deep frying pan to about 365°F (190°C). If you don't have a frying thermometer, test the oil temperature by dropping a small piece of bread into the hot oil. If the bread bubbles to the surface and begins to turn golden, the oil is ready.

5. Fry the samosas in small batches until golden brown and crisp, 5–7 minutes each batch. Scoop out with a slotted spoon and drain well on paper towels. Serve hot.

ONION focaccia

1	recipe Basic Dough (see page 28)
3	tablespoons extra-virgin olive oil
2	large red onions, thinly sliced
	Salt and freshly ground black pepper
1	tablespoon cider vinegar
1/2	cup (60 g) freshly grated pecorino or Parmesan cheese
1	teaspoon red pepper flakes

Serves 6–8 • Preparation 30 minutes + 1¾ hours to rise • Cooking 35–40 minutes • Difficulty 2

1. Prepare the basic dough and set aside to rise.

2. Preheat the oven to 425°F (220°C/gas 7). Oil an 11 x 17-inch (28 x 45-cm) rimmed baking sheet. Put the dough on the sheet, stretching to fit. Drizzle with 1 tablespoon of oil. Cover with a clean towel and let sit for 15 minutes.

3. Heat the remaining 2 tablespoons of oil in a frying pan over low heat. Add the onions, season with salt and pepper, then simmer, stirring occasionally, until the onions are tender and golden brown, 12–15 minutes. Stir in the vinegar.

4. Top the dough with the cheese, onion mixture, and red pepper flakes. Bake for 20–25 minutes, until golden brown. Serve warm or at room temperature.

LEMON & PARMESAN *pizza*

1   recipe Basic Dough
(see page 28)

5   ounces (150 g) Parmesan
cheese, shaved

10   very thin slices unwaxed
lemon, with peel, seeds
removed

1   sweet red onion, very thinly
sliced

1   tablespoon small sprigs fresh
rosemary

      Freshly ground black pepper

2   tablespoons extra-virgin olive
oil, to drizzle

Serves 6–8 • Preparation 30 minutes + 1½ hours to rise • Cooking 10–15 minutes • Difficulty 2

1. Prepare the basic dough and set aside to rise.

2. Preheat the oven to 425°F (220°C/gas 7). Oil two 12-inch (30-cm) pizza stones or pans. Divide the dough in half and roll and stretch each piece to fit the pans.

3. Arrange the cheese evenly over the dough, leaving a 1-inch (2.5-cm) border around the edges. Top with the lemon and onion slices. Sprinkle with the rosemary and season with pepper. Drizzle with the oil.

4. Bake for 10–15 minutes, until bubbling and golden brown. Slice into wedges and serve hot.

Some people like a thick, bread-like pizza crust, while others prefer a thin, crisp crust that bakes to a snappy finish. It's a question of taste. You can use our basic dough to make a very large pizza with a thin crust, or a smaller one with a deeper, doughier finish. It's up to you, just roll or stretch the dough to the preferred size and thickness (remember it will shrink a little during baking).

GREEK pizza

Basic Dough
1 ounce (30 g) fresh yeast or 2 ($^1/_4$-ounce/7-g) packages active dry yeast
$1^1/_2$ cups (370 ml) warm water
3 cups (450 g) strong white bread flour
$^1/_2$ teaspoon salt

Topping
4 medium plum tomatoes
1 clove garlic, coarsely chopped
2 tablespoons extra-virgin olive oil
Salt and freshly ground black pepper
4 ounces (120 g) freshly grated halloumi cheese
2 tablespoons pine nuts
1 cup (50 g) baby arugula (rocket)
1 tablespoon balsamic vinegar
$^1/_4$ cup pitted kalamata olives, coarsely chopped

Serves 4-6 • Preparation 30 minutes + $1^1/_2$ hours to rise • Cooking 10-15 minutes • Difficulty 2

Basic Dough
1. Place the yeast in a small bowl. Add $^1/_2$ cup (120 ml) of the warm water and stir until the yeast has dissolved. Set aside until foamy, 10-15 minutes.
2. Combine the flour and salt in a large bowl. Make a well in the center and pour in the yeast mixture and enough of the remaining water to obtain a moist, kneadable dough. Stir until the flour has almost all been absorbed, then turn out onto a lightly floured work surface and knead until smooth and elastic, 10-15 minutes. Shape into a ball and place in an oiled bowl. Set aside in a warm place until doubled in bulk, about $1^1/_2$ hours.

Topping
1. Preheat the oven to 450°F (220°C/gas 9). Oil a large baking sheet or pizza stone or pan.
2. Combine the tomatoes, garlic, and 1 tablespoon of oil in a food processor. Season with salt and pepper. Pulse until just incorporated but still chunky.
3. Roll and stretch the dough on a floured work surface to the desired size and thickness. Transfer to the prepared baking sheet. Spread with the tomato sauce, leaving a 1-inch (2.5-cm) border around the edges. Top with the cheese and pine nuts.
4. Bake for 15-20 minutes, until golden brown. Toss the arugula, vinegar, olives, and remaining 1 tablespoon of oil in a bowl. Sprinkle over the pizza and serve hot.

soups & salads

SPICY GARBANZO BEAN soup

2   tablespoons extra-virgin olive oil
1   medium onion, coarsely chopped
4   cloves garlic, finely chopped
3   stalks celery, coarsely chopped
2   teaspoons ground cumin
1   fresh red chili, seeded and thinly sliced
3   cups (750 ml) hot vegetable stock
1   (14-ounce/400-g) can chopped plum tomatoes, with juice
1   (14-ounce/400-g) can garbanzo beans (chickpeas), rinsed and drained
    Freshly ground black pepper
1   cup (150 g) frozen peas
2   tablespoons freshly squeezed lemon juice
    Salt
1   tablespoon finely grated unwaxed lemon zest
1/4 cup fresh cilantro (coriander) leaves
    Flatbread, to serve

Serves 4–6 • Preparation 15 minutes • Cooking 25 minutes • Difficulty 1

1. Heat the oil in a large soup pot over medium-low heat. Add the onion, garlic, and celery and sauté until softened, about 10 minutes. Add the cumin and chili and sauté for 1 minute.

2. Turn up the heat, add the vegetable stock, tomatoes, and garbanzo beans, and season generously with black pepper. Simmer for 10 minutes. Add the peas and lemon juice and simmer for 5 more minutes.

3. Season with salt and pepper. Sprinkle with the lemon zest and cilantro. Ladle into bowls, and serve hot with the flatbread.

If you liked this recipe, you will love these as well.

SPICY PASTA
soup

LENTIL & SWEET POTATO soup

BEAN & ORANGE
salad

Peas are a good source of vegetarian protein and a very good source of dietary fiber and vitamin C. The potatoes in this recipe provide a creamy, comforting texture, making it perfect for winter evenings!

CREAMY PEA & POTATO soup

2	tablespoons extra-virgin olive oil
1	medium onion, finely chopped
2	pounds (1 kg) potatoes, peeled and cut into small chunks
5	cups (1.25 liters) vegetable stock
3	cups (450 g) frozen peas
1/2	cup coarsely chopped fresh mint + extra leaves, to garnish
	Salt and freshly ground black pepper
	Freshly baked bread, to serve

Serves 4–6 • Preparation 15 minutes • Cooking 15–20 minutes
Difficulty 1

1. Heat the oil in a large soup pot over medium heat. Add the onion and sauté until softened, 3–4 minutes. Add the potatoes and vegetable stock and bring to a boil. Cover and simmer until tender, 10–15 minutes. Add the peas 2 minutes before the end of the cooking time.

2. Use a slotted spoon to remove a quarter of the vegetables from the pan and set aside. Chop the remaining vegetables and stock in a food processor or with a hand-held blender until smooth.

3. Stir in the reserved vegetables and chopped mint. Season with salt and pepper. Ladle into soup bowls and serve hot, garnished with extra mint, and with the bread on the side.

If you liked this recipe, you will love these as well.

RICE & CELERY
soup

SWEET POTATO
soup

VEGETABLE
chowder

TOMATO soup

Serves 4-6 • Preparation 15 minutes • Cooking 18-20 minutes • Difficulty 1

2	tablespoons extra-virgin olive oil	2	(14-ounce/400-g) cans chopped tomatoes, with juice
2	onions, finely chopped		
2	carrots, grated	2	cups (500 ml) vegetable stock
2	stalks celery, chopped		
2	cloves garlic, finely chopped	1/4	cup (60 ml) sour cream
		1/2	cup finely chopped fresh basil

1. Heat the oil in a soup pot over medium heat. Add the onions, carrots, celery, and garlic and sauté until softened, 3-4 minutes. Add the tomatoes and vegetable stock. Simmer for 15 minutes.

2. Remove from the heat and purée with a hand-held blender. Ladle into bowls, garnish with a dollop of sour cream and some basil, and serve hot.

RICE & CELERY soup

Serves 6 • Preparation 15 minutes • Cooking 30-35 minutes Difficulty 1

3	tablespoons butter	1	bay leaf
2	tablespoons extra-virgin olive oil	5	cups (1.25 liters) vegetable stock
8	ounces (250 g) celery stalks, fairly finely chopped		Salt
		1 1/4	cups (250 g) short-grain rice
2	tablespoons finely chopped fresh parsley		Freshly grated Parmesan cheese

1. Put 2 tablespoons of butter and the oil in a soup pot over low heat. Add the celery, parsley, and bay leaf and simmer, stirring often, until tender, 10-15 minutes.

2. Turn the heat up to medium and add the vegetable stock. Season with salt and bring to a boil. Simmer for 5 minutes.

3. Add the rice and simmer until tender, about 15 minutes. Remove the bay leaf and stir in the remaining 1 tablespoon of butter.

4. Ladle into soup bowls, and serve hot sprinkled with Parmesan.

CHILLED avocado soup

Serves 4 • Preparation 15 minutes + 2 hours to chill Difficulty 1

3	ripe avocados	1	tablespoon freshly squeezed lime juice
2	cups (500 ml) chilled low-fat milk		
		1/2	teaspoon coarse sea salt
1/3	cup (40 g) walnut halves		
		1	cup (250 ml) iced water
1/3	cup fresh cilantro (coriander) leaves + extra, to garnish		
		1	medium tomato, finely chopped
1	small onion, finely chopped		

1. Halve and pit two avocados. Scoop out the flesh with a spoon and place in a blender. Add the milk, walnuts, cilantro, onion, lime juice, salt, and water and chop until smooth.

2. Cover and refrigerate until the soup is well chilled, at least two hours.

3. Halve and pit the remaining avocado. Cut into small chunks. Ladle the soup into bowls, garnish with diced avocado, tomato, and cilantro, and serve.

SWEET POTATO soup

Serves 6 • Preparation 15 minutes • Cooking 25-30 minutes Difficulty 2

2	teaspoons curry powder	1	teaspoon finely grated ginger
1/4	cup (60 ml) extra-virgin olive oil		Salt and freshly ground black pepper
2	onions, grated	2	pounds (1 kg) sweet potatoes, peeled and grated
1	eating apple, peeled, cored, and grated		
3	cloves garlic, finely chopped	5	cups (1.25 liters) vegetable stock
1/2	cup coarsely chopped fresh cilantro (coriander)	1	cup (180 g) red lentils
		1 1/4	cups (300 ml) milk
			Freshly squeezed juice of 1 lime

1. Put the curry powder in a soup pot over medium heat and toast for 1-2 minutes. Stir in the oil, then add the onions, apple, garlic, cilantro stalks, and ginger. Season with salt and pepper, then simmer for 5 minutes, stirring often.

2. Add the sweet potatoes to the pan with the stock, lentils, and milk. Cover and simmer for 20 minutes.

3. Chop until smooth with a hand-held blender. Stir in the lime juice, and serve hot garnished with the cilantro.

TUSCAN BAKED MINESTRONE (ribollita)

1	onion, finely chopped
4	tablespoons (60 ml) extra-virgin olive oil
1	(14-ounce/400-g) can cannellini beans
4	cups (1 liter) vegetable stock
1/2	small Savoy cabbage, shredded
3	small tomatoes, coarsely chopped
8	ounces (250 g) Swiss Chard (silverbeet), shredded
1	zucchini (courgette), coarsely chopped
1	carrot, sliced
1	stalk celery, coarsely chopped
2	potatoes, diced
8	ounces (250 g) Tuscan (black) kale, shredded
1	leek, sliced
	Salt and freshly ground black pepper
6	slices firm-textured whole-wheat (wholemeal) bread

Serves 4–6 • Preparation 30 minutes • Cooking 1½ hours • Difficulty 2

1. Heat 2 tablespoons of oil in a soup pot. Add the onion and sauté until softened, 3–4 minutes. Purée two-thirds of the cannellini beans in a food processor. Add the puréed beans and stock to the onion. Add all the remaining vegetables and simmer until tender, at least 1 hour.

2. Preheat the oven to 350°F (180°C/gas 4). Stir the remaining beans into the soup and season with salt and pepper.

3. Arrange the bread in an oiled baking dish and ladle the vegetable soup over the top. Drizzle with the remaining 2 tablespoons of oil and bake for 20 minutes. Serve hot.

SPICY PASTA soup

2   tablespoons extra-virgin
    olive oil
1   red onion, finely chopped
1   red chili, seeded and finely
    sliced
2   (14-ounce/400-g) cans whole
    plum tomatoes, with juice
4   cups (1 liter) vegetable stock
4   ounces (120 g) farfalline pasta
    (small bowtie pasta)
4   tablespoons chopped pitted
    black olives
1/4 cup coarsely chopped fresh
    basil
4   tablespoons pesto

Serves 4 • Preparation 15 minutes • Cooking 15–20 minutes • Difficulty 1

1. Heat the oil in a large soup pot over medium heat. Add the
    onion and chili, and sauté until softened, 3–4 minutes. Stir in
    the tomatoes and vegetable stock. Cover, bring to a boil,
    then remove the lid and simmer for 5 minutes.

2. Add the pasta and simmer until just al dente, 6–8 minutes
    (depending on the size of the pasta). Stir in the olives and
    basil and remove from the heat.

3. Ladle into bowls, and serve hot drizzled with the pesto.

A vegetable chowder is a thickened soup. Corn and potatoes are traditional ingredients, but you can add-lib with the rest according to what you like and have on hand.

VEGETABLE chowder

3	tablespoons butter
1	large onion, diced
2	medium red bell peppers (capsicums), seeded and diced
$^1/_2$	teaspoon dried thyme
3	cups (750 ml) milk
$2^1/_2$	pounds (1.25 kg) baking potatoes, peeled and cut into small cubes
5	cups (1.25 liters) cold water
8	ears (cobs) corn, kernels removed (about 4 cups)
	Salt and freshly ground black pepper
1	pounds (500 g) green beans, trimmed and cut into short lengths

Serves 6–8 • Preparation 20 minutes • Cooking 30–35 minutes
Difficulty 1

1. Melt the butter in a large soup pot over medium heat. Add the onion, bell peppers, and thyme and cook, stirring occasionally, until the vegetables are softened, 8–10 minutes.

2. Add the milk, potatoes, and water. Bring to a boil, then cover and simmer on low heat until the potatoes are almost tender, 8–10 minutes.

3. Stir in the corn and season with salt and pepper. Simmer until the corn is tender, 3–5 minutes.

4. Transfer 3 cups of the soup to a food processor and chop until smooth.

5. Return to the pot and add the green beans. Bring to a simmer and cook until the beans are tender, 5–8 minutes. Check the seasoning, ladle into bowls, and serve hot.

If you liked this recipe, you will love these as well.

CREAMY PEA & POTATO
soup

TOMATO
soup

RICE & CELERY
soup

LENTIL & SWEET POTATO soup

2 tablespoons extra-virgin olive oil

1 medium onion, chopped

2 medium carrots, chopped

2 stalks celery, chopped

1 bay leaf

1 clove garlic, finely chopped

1½ teaspoons curry powder

7 cups (1.75 liters) water

2 cups (300 g) brown lentils

2 medium sweet potatoes (about 1 pound/500 g), peeled and cut in small cubes

2 cups (500 g) vegetable stock

8 ounces (250 g) green beans, cut into short lengths

1 (14-ounce/400-g) can diced tomatoes, with juice

½ cup chopped fresh cilantro leaves

Salt and black pepper

Low-fat yogurt, to serve

Serves 6–8 • Preparation 20 minutes • Cooking 30 minutes • Difficulty 1

1. Heat the oil in a soup pot over medium-high heat. Add the onion, carrots, celery, and bay leaf and sauté until softened, 5–7 minutes. Add the garlic and curry powder and cook until fragrant, about 1 minute.

2. Add the water and lentils. Bring to a boil, then cover and simmer over low heat for 10 minutes. Add the sweet potatoes and vegetable stock and simmer until the lentils and potatoes are just tender, about 15 minutes.

3. Add the green beans and tomatoes. Cook until warmed through, 2–4 minutes. Remove the bay leaf. Add the cilantro; season with salt and pepper, and serve hot with the yogurt.

CABBAGE SOUP with garlic crostini

6   large slices firm-textured bread

$1/3$ cup (90 ml) extra-virgin olive oil

2   cloves garlic

1   medium Savoy cabbage

6   cups (1.5 liters) vegetable stock

$1/2$ cup (60 g) freshly grated Parmesan cheese

   Salt and freshly ground black pepper

1. Discard the tough outer leaves from the cabbage. Chop the rest into wedges and boil in lightly salted water until tender, 5–7 minutes. Drain and chop finely.

2. Heat the vegetable stock in a large soup pot and add the cabbage. Bring to a boil over medium heat and simmer for 10 minutes.

3. Cut each slice of bread in three. Heat the oil in a large frying pan over medium heat. Add the garlic and bread and fry until golden brown on both sides. Remove from the heat and drain on paper towels.

4. Ladle the soup into bowls. Sprinkle with the cheese and garnish with the garlic crostini. Serve hot.

Whip up this salad during the winter months when oranges are in season and many other fresh salad vegetables are less easy to find. White beans are a good source of lean protein, they are low in fat, and packed with dietary fiber. Combined with the fresh green salad and oranges, they make a healthy light lunch or supper.

BEAN & ORANGE salad

8	ounces (250 g) green beans, trimmed and halved
2	large juicy oranges
1/4	cup (60 ml) extra-virgin olive oil
2	tablespoons white wine vinegar
	Salt and freshly ground black pepper
7	ounces (200 g) feta cheese, crumbled
1	head romaine lettuce, halved and coarsely chopped
1	small red onion, halved and thinly sliced
1	(14-ounce/400-g) can white beans, rinsed and drained

Serves 4–6 • Preparation 15 minutes • Cooking 4–5 minutes • Difficulty 1

1. Cook the green beans in a pan of lightly salted boiling water until just tender, 4–5 minutes. Drain well and set aside in the colander to cool a little while you prepare the orange.

2. Slice off both ends of each orange. Cut off the peel, following the curve of the fruit. Halve the fruit from top to bottom, and remove all the white pith.

3. Whisk the oil and vinegar in a small bowl. Season with salt and pepper.

4. Put the feta, oranges, lettuce, onion, white beans, and green beans in a salad bowl. Toss to combine, and serve.

If you liked this recipe, you will love these as well.

SPICY GARBANZO BEAN soup

BLACK BEAN chili

TUSCAN CANNELLINI bean stew

CHEESE & BULGUR salad

Serves 4 • Preparation 15 minutes + 30 minutes to stand
Difficulty 1

1⅓	cups (250 g) medium-grind bulgur	2	shallots, very finely chopped
	Salt and freshly ground black pepper	2	tablespoons red wine vinegar
4	cups (1 liter) boiling water	¼	cup (60 ml) extra-virgin olive oil
24	cherry tomatoes, halved	5	ounces (150 g) fresh goat cheese, crumbled
2	cups (100 g) finely chopped fresh parsley		

1. Mix the bulgur in a bowl with ½ teaspoon of salt and the boiling water. Cover and let stand until tender but still slightly chewy, about 30 minutes.

2. Drain the bulgur, pressing to remove excess liquid. Place in a salad bowl. Add the tomatoes, parsley, shallots, vinegar, and oil. Season with salt and pepper, and toss gently. Top with the cheese and serve.

COUSCOUS salad

Serves 4–6 • Preparation 15 minutes + 30 minutes to stand
Difficulty 1

2½	cups (250 g) couscous	1	cucumber, diced
2	cups (500 ml) boiling vegetable stock	5	ounces (150 g) feta cheese, crumbled
4	scallions (spring onions), trimmed and sliced	½	teaspoon ground cumin
		⅓	cup (90 ml) pesto
1	red bell pepper (capsicum), seeded and sliced	4	tablespoons toasted pine nuts
		2	tablespoons golden raisins (sultanas)
1	green bell pepper (capsicum), seeded and sliced	½	cup coarsely chopped fresh cilantro (coriander)

1. Put the couscous in a large bowl and pour in the vegetable stock. Cover, then leave for 10 minutes, until fluffy and all the stock has been absorbed.

2. Add the scallions, bell peppers, cucumber, pesto, cumin, feta, pine nuts, and cilantro. Toss gently and serve.

POTATO SALAD with egg

Serves 4 • Preparation 15 minutes • Cooking 15 minutes
Difficulty 1

6	tablespoons (90 ml) extra-virgin olive oil		mustard
		2	shallots, chopped
1	pound (500 g) potatoes, cubed	2	pounds (1 kg) spinach, tough stems removed, chopped
	Salt and freshly ground black pepper		
2	tablespoons red wine vinegar	2	ounces (60 g) Parmesan cheese, in flakes
1	tablespoon Dijon	4	large eggs

1. Heat 3 tablespoons of the oil in a large frying pan over medium heat. Add the potatoes, season with salt and pepper, and cook until tender and browned, 12–15 minutes.

2. Whisk the remaining 3 tablespoons of oil in a large bowl with the vinegar, mustard, shallots, salt, and pepper. Add the spinach and Parmesan. Set aside without tossing.

3. Add the cooked potatoes to the spinach mixture. Toss gently, then divide among four plates.

4. Heat the frying pan over medium heat. Fry the eggs. Season with salt and pepper. Top each salad with a fried egg, and serve hot.

LENTIL & BULGUR salad

Serves 4–6 • Preparation 15 minutes + 30 minutes to stand
Cooking 15–20 minutes • Difficulty 1

1	cup (180 g) green Le Puy lentils, rinsed		halved
		6	scallions (spring onions), thinly sliced
1	cup (250 ml) water		
1	cup (200 g) fine-grain bulgur	¼	cup (60 ml) freshly squeezed lime juice
1	cup (250 ml) water	3	tablespoons extra-virgin olive oil
	Salt and freshly ground black pepper	4	ounces (120 g) feta cheese, crumbled
20	cherry tomatoes,		

1. Put the lentils in a medium saucepan and cover with 1 inch (2.5 cm) of water. Bring to a boil, then cover and simmer until the lentils are tender, 15–20 minutes. Drain well.

2. Bring the water to a boil in a small saucepan. Stir in the bulgur, ½ teaspoon salt, and ¼ teaspoon pepper. Cover, remove from the heat, and let stand until the liquid is absorbed, about 30 minutes.

3. Transfer the bulgur to a large bowl. Gently stir in the lentils, tomatoes, scallions, lemon juice, oil, and feta. Toss gently and serve.

Don't be tempted to cool the pasta under cold running water as this will remove so much of its delicious flavor. Just drain it well and place in a clean, lightly oiled bowl. Add the other salad ingredients, toss well, and serve.

GREEK pasta salad

1	pound (500 g) penne
7	ounces (200 g) feta cheese, cut into small cubes.
2	cups (100 g) large black kalamata olives
2	small sweet red onions, finely chopped
2	cloves garlic, finely chopped
24	cherry tomatoes, halved
1	cucumber, cut in small cubes
2	tablespoons finely chopped fresh mint + extra leaves, to garnish
4	tablespoons coarsely chopped fresh basil + extra leaves, to garnish
2	tablespoons brine-cured capers, drained
1	tablespoon finely chopped unwaxed lemon zest, yellow part only
1/4	cup (60 ml) extra-virgin olive oil

Serves 4-6 • Preparation 20 minutes • Cooking 12 minutes • Difficulty 1

1. Cook the pasta in a large pot of salted boiling water until al dente, about 12 minutes. Drain and place in a large, lightly oiled salad bowl.

2. Add the feta, olives, onions, garlic, cherry tomatoes, cucumber, mint, basil, capers, and lemon zest and toss gently. The cheese will melt a little into the warm pasta. Drizzle with the oil, garnish with the extra mint and basil leaves, and serve.

If you liked this recipe, you will love these as well.

PASTA SALAD with eggplant & pine nuts

PASTA SALAD with blue cheese & cumin

FUSILLI with goat cheese & tomatoes

PASTA SALAD with eggplant & pine nuts

1	large eggplant (aubergine), with skin, cut into $1/2$-inch (1-cm) thick slices
1	tablespoon coarse sea salt
2	cups (500 ml) olive oil, for frying
2	yellow bell peppers (capsicums)
6	tablespoons (90 ml) extra-virgin olive oil
1	medium onion, finely chopped
2	cloves garlic, finely chopped
$1/8$	teaspoon salt
2	tablespoons pine nuts
1	pound (500 g) short pasta (such as ridged ditalini)
2	tablespoons salt-cured capers, rinsed
1	cup (100 g) green olives, pitted and coarsely chopped
1	small bunch fresh basil, torn
2	tablespoons finely chopped fresh parsley
1	tablespoon finely chopped fresh oregano

Serves 4–6 • Preparation 30 minutes + 1 hour to drain the eggplant
Cooking 20–30 minutes • Difficulty 2

1. Place the eggplant in a colander and sprinkle with the coarse sea salt. Let drain for 1 hour. Chop into cubes. Heat the frying oil in a large deep frying pan until very hot. Fry the eggplant in small batches until golden brown. Drain on paper towels.

2. Preheat an overhead broiler (grill). Broil the bell peppers until the skins are blackened. Wrap in a plastic bag for 10 minutes, then remove the skins and seeds. Cut into squares.

3. Heat 3 tablespoons of extra-virgin oil in a small saucepan over medium heat. Add the onion, garlic, and salt and sauté until golden. Dry-fry the pine nuts in a frying pan over medium heat until crisp and golden, 3–4 minutes.

4. Cook the pasta in a large pot of salted boiling water until al dente. Drain well and place in a large, lightly oiled salad bowl. Add the eggplant, capers, bell peppers, onion mixture, pine nuts, olives, basil, and oregano. Toss well, and serve.

PASTA SALAD with blue cheese & cumin

1	pound (500 g) farfalle pasta
7	ounces (200 g) blue cheese (such as Roquefort, Danish, or Gorgonzola), crumbled or cut into small cubes.
1	cup (100 g) large black olives
1	small sweet red onion, finely chopped
2	cloves garlic, finely chopped
20	cherry tomatoes, halved
$^1/_2$	cup coarsely chopped fresh cilantro (coriander)
2	tablespoons brined-cured capers, drained
$^1/_2$	teaspoon ground cumin
2	cups (100 g) arugula (rocket)
1	cup (120 g) coarsely chopped walnuts
$^1/_4$	cup (60 ml) extra-virgin olive oil

Serves 4–6 • Preparation 15 minutes • Cooking 12 minutes • Difficulty 1

1. Cook the pasta in a large pot of salted boiling water until al dente. Drain well and place in a large, lightly oiled salad bowl.

2. Add the blue cheese, olives, onion, garlic, cherry tomatoes, cilantro, capers, and cumin and toss gently. The cheese will melt into the warm pasta.

3. Dry-fry the walnuts in a large frying pan over medium heat until crisp and golden, 3–4 minutes.

4. Add the arugula, walnuts, and oil to the salad bowl, toss gently again, and serve.

This is an old Tuscan recipe and a great way to use up yesterday's leftover bread. In Tuscany, it is made with the local firm-textured unsalted white bread. Traditionally, panzanella does not include beans and cheese, but we have added them to make a more substantial main course salad.

PANZANELLA

¹/₄ cup (60 ml) red wine vinegar

¹/₃ cup (90 ml) extra-virgin olive oil

Salt and freshly ground black pepper

1 (14-ounce/400-g) can cannellini beans, rinsed and drained

8 ounces (250 g) firm-textured whole-wheat (wholemeal) bread, torn into small pieces

1 pound (500 g) plum tomatoes, coarsely chopped

1 cucumber, thinly sliced

1 small red onion, thinly sliced

5 ounces (150 g) aged pecorino cheese, diced

¹/₄ cup fresh basil leaves, torn

Serves 4 • Preparation 15 minutes + 1–2 hours to chill • Difficulty 1

1. Whisk the vinegar and oil in a large bowl. Season with salt and pepper.

2. Add the cannellini beans, bread, tomatoes, cucumber, onion, and cheese. Toss to combine.

3. Cover and chill for 1–2 hours. Stir in the basil and serve.

If you liked this recipe, you will love these as well.

TUSCAN BAKED MINESTRONE (ribollita)

CHEESE & BULGUR salad

COUSCOUS salad

BULGUR SALAD with feta & cherry tomatoes

1   cup (180 g) medium-grind bulgur

     Salt and freshly ground black pepper

2   cups (500 ml) boiling water

4   tablespoons pine nuts

2   tablespoons freshly squeezed lemon juice

2   tablespoons extra-virgin olive oil

5   ounces (150 g) feta cheese, crumbled

2   small red onions, thinly sliced

1   cup (50 g) finely chopped fresh parsley

1   cucumber, diced

16   cherry tomatoes, halved

4   cups (200 g) baby salad greens

Serves 4–6 • Preparation 15 minutes + 30 minutes to soak • Difficulty 1

1. Mix the bulgur with ½ teaspoon of salt and the boiling water. Cover and set aside until tender, about 30 minutes.

2. Dry-fry the pine nuts in a small frying pan over medium heat until golden, 3–4 minutes. Whisk the lemon juice and oil in a small bowl. Season with salt and pepper.

3. Drain the bulgur, pressing to remove excess liquid. Place in a bowl. Add the feta, onions, parsley, cucumber, and half the dressing. Season with salt and pepper.

4. Toss the salad greens separately with the remaining dressing. Place in serving bowls, top with the bulgur mixture and pine nuts, and serve.

QUINOA SALAD with celery & almonds

½ cup (60 g) coarsely chopped almonds
1 cup (180 g) quinoa
3 tablespoons extra-virgin olive oil
1 yellow bell pepper (capsicum), seeded, cut into small pieces
4 cloves garlic, finely chopped
4 scallions (spring onions), thinly sliced
½ teaspoon red pepper flakes
1 tablespoon finely chopped fresh thyme
2 cups (500 ml) water
½ teaspoon coarse sea salt
2 medium zucchini (courgettes), cut into small cubes
3 stalks celery, diced
2 limes, halved

Serves 4 • Preparation 15 minutes • Cooking 15–20 minutes • Difficulty 1

1. Preheat the oven to 350°F (180°C/gas 4). Toast the almonds until crisp and golden, 5–7 minutes. Set aside.

2. Rinse the quinoa under cold running water until the water runs clear. Drain well.

3. Heat 2 tablespoons of oil in a saucepan over medium heat. Add the bell pepper, garlic, scallions, and red pepper flakes and sauté until the bell pepper is tender, about 5 minutes.

4. Stir in the quinoa, thyme, water, and salt. Bring to a boil, then cover and simmer for 7 minutes. Stir in the zucchini, then simmer until the quinoa is tender, about 5 more minutes. Remove from the heat.

5. Stir in the celery, almonds, and remaining 1 tablespoon of oil. Season with salt, and fluff with a fork. Let cool a little, then drizzle with lime juice, and serve.

Delicious Le Puy green lentils come from the Auvergne region of central France. They do not require soaking and can be cooked in 15-20 minutes. Like all lentils, they are packed with protein, dietary fiber, vitamins, and trace minerals, making them a very healthy food choice. Le Puy green lentils are especially suitable for salads, since they hold their shape so well during cooking.

WARM LENTIL & GOAT CHEESE salad

1	cup (180 g) Le Puy green lentils
4	tablespoons (60 ml) extra-virgin olive oil
3	shallots, thinly sliced
1	carrot, cut into small cubes
1	stalk celery, cut into small cubes
1	red bell pepper (capsicum), seeded and diced
4	tablespoons coarsely chopped fresh parsley
2	tablespoons balsamic vinegar
3	cups (150 g) baby spinach leaves
	Salt and freshly ground black pepper
5	ounces (150 g) fresh goat cheese

Serves 4 • Preparation 15 minutes • Cooking 15–20 minutes • Difficulty 1

1. Bring a medium saucepan of water to a boil. Add the lentils, and simmer, stirring occasionally, until tender, 15-20 minutes.

2. Heat 2 tablespoons of the oil in a large frying pan over medium heat. Add the shallots and sauté until beginning to soften, 2-3 minutes. Add the carrot, celery, and bell pepper and continue to cook, stirring occasionally, until the vegetables are tender, about 5 minutes. Stir in the parsley, balsamic vinegar, and remaining 1 tablespoon of oil. Transfer to a large bowl.

3. Drain the lentils and add to bowl with the vegetables. Stir in the spinach leaves and season with salt and pepper. Crumble the goat cheese over the top, toss gently to combine, and serve warm.

If you liked this recipe, you will love these as well.

SWEET POTATO soup

LENTIL & SWEET POTATO soup

SPICY VEGETARIAN bake

pasta & grains

BUCATINI with tomato & almond sauce

4   tablespoons (60 ml) extra-
      virgin olive oil
1   large onion, finely chopped
1½   pounds (750 g) tomatoes,
      peeled and coarsely chopped
      Salt and freshly ground black
      pepper
1   cup (120 g) peeled almonds
4   slices day-old, firm-textured
      bread, cut in tiny cubes
1   pound (500 g) bucatini
½   cup (60 g) freshly grated
      pecorino or Parmesan cheese
      Fresh basil, to garnish

Serves 4–6 • Preparation 15 minutes • Cooking 30 minutes • Difficulty 1

1. Heat 2 tablespoons of oil in a medium saucepan over medium heat. Add the onion and sauté until softened, 3–4 minutes. Add the tomatoes and season with salt and pepper. Cover and simmer over low heat for 20–25 minutes.

2. Dry-fry the almonds in a small frying pan over medium-low heat until crisp and golden brown, 4–5 minutes. Set aside.

3. Heat the remaining 2 tablespoons of oil in a large frying pan over medium-high heat. Add the bread and toss until crisp and golden brown, 2–3 minutes.

4. Cook the bucatini in a large pot of salted boiling water until al dente, 12–15 minutes. Drain and transfer to a heated serving bowl.

5. Pour the tomato sauce over the top. Sprinkle with the almonds, bread, and cheese, and toss gently. Serve hot, garnished with the basil.

If you liked this recipe, you will love these as well.

RIGATONI with roasted
bell pepper sauce

TAGLIATELLE
with almonds

HOT & SPICY
spaghetti

FARFALLE with grilled veggies

1	red bell pepper (capsicum), seeded and sliced
1	yellow bell pepper (capsicum), seeded and sliced
1	green bell pepper (capsicum), seeded and sliced
1	eggplant (aubergine), with skin, thinly sliced
3	zucchini (courgettes), thinly sliced lengthwise
1	pound (500 g) farfalle
1/2	cup coarsely chopped fresh basil
1	tablespoon finely chopped fresh mint
1	clove garlic, finely chopped
	Salt and freshly ground black pepper
1/4	cup (60 ml) extra-virgin olive oil

Serves 4–6 • Preparation 30 minutes • Cooking 20–30 minutes
Difficulty 2

1. Preheat the broiler (grill) and broil the bell peppers, turning often, until the skins are blackened. Wrap in a plastic bag or aluminum foil for 10 minutes. Unwrap and remove the skins and seeds. Chop coarsely.

2. Preheat a grill pan (griddle) over medium-high heat. Add the eggplant and zucchini and cook until tender and marked with black lines. Chop coarsely.

3. Cook the pasta in a large pot of salted boiling water until al dente, 10–12 minutes. Drain well and place in a large bowl. Add the grilled vegetables and toss gently. Add the basil, mint, and garlic. Season with salt and pepper, drizzle with the oil, and serve hot.

FUSILLI with goat cheese & tomatoes

1	pound (500 g) fusilli
2	cloves garlic, finely chopped
$1/4$	cup (60 ml) extra-virgin olive oil
$1^1/_2$	pounds (750 g) cherry tomatoes, halved
1	cup (100 g) black olives
2	tablespoons brine-cured capers, drained
	Freshly ground black pepper
8	ounces (250 g) fresh, creamy goat cheese
$1/2$	cup fresh basil leaves

Serves 4–6 • Preparation 15 minutes • Cooking 15–20 minutes
Difficulty 1

1. Cook the pasta in a large pot of salted boiling water until al dente, 10–12 minutes.

2. Heat the oil in a large frying pan over medium heat. Add the garlic and sauté until pale gold, 2–3 minutes. Add the tomatoes, olives, and capers. Season with pepper. Cook over high heat for 2–3 minutes, stirring often.

3. Drain the pasta and add to the pan with the tomatoes. Stir in the goat cheese and basil, tossing gently. Serve hot.

Bell peppers, or capsicums, as they are known in many parts of the world, are always a healthy food choice. They are a very good source of dietary fiber, vitamins A, C, K, and B6, potassium, and manganese, and a good source of thiamin, niacin, folate, magnesium, and copper, as well as many trace elements and antioxidants.

RIGATONI with roasted bell pepper sauce

2	large red bell peppers (capsicums)
1	large yellow bell pepper (capsicum)
$1/4$	cup (60 ml) extra-virgin olive oil
1	pound (500 g) rigatoni
$1\frac{1}{2}$	pounds (750 g) tomatoes, peeled and sliced
2	cloves garlic, finely chopped
2	tablespoons finely chopped fresh parsley
4	tablespoons freshly grated pecorino or Parmesan cheese + extra, to serve
	Salt and freshly ground black pepper

Serves 4-6 • Preparation 30 minutes • Cooking 30-35 minutes Difficulty 2

1. Preheat an overhead broiler (grill) and broil the bell peppers, turning often, until the skins are blackened. Wrap in a plastic bag or aluminum foil for 10 minutes. Unwrap and remove the skins and seeds. Chop into small strips.

2. Heat the oil in a large frying pan over medium heat. Add the tomatoes, garlic, and parsley. Season with salt and pepper and simmer over low heat for 20-30 minutes.

3. Cook the rigatoni in a large pan of salted boiling water until al dente, 10-12 minutes. Drain the pasta and add to the pan with the sauce. Add the bell peppers and cheese and stir gently. Serve hot, with extra cheese sprinkled on top.

If you liked this recipe, you will love these as well.

FARFALLE with grilled veggies

CONCHIGLIE with cauliflower

ORECCHIETTE with broccoli

CONCHIGLIE with cauliflower

Serves 4–6 • Preparation 20 minutes • Cooking 20–30 minutes • Difficulty 1

1/4	cup (60 ml) extra-virgin olive oil		Salt and freshly ground black pepper
2	cloves garlic, finely chopped	1	medium cauliflower, broken into florets
1 1/2	pounds (750 g) tomatoes, peeled and chopped	1	pound (500 g) conchiglie
3	tablespoons finely chopped fresh basil + extra, to garnish	1/2	cup (60 g) freshly grated Parmesan cheese

1. Heat the oil in a large frying pan over medium heat. Add the garlic and sauté until pale gold, 2–3 minutes. Add the tomatoes and basil, season with salt and pepper, and simmer over low heat for 20 minutes.

2. Bring a large pot of salted water to a boil over high heat. Add the cauliflower and pasta and cook until the pasta is al dente, 10–12 minutes. Drain well.

3. Add the pasta and cauliflower to the sauce and toss gently. Sprinkle with the cheese, garnish with the extra basil, and serve hot.

PENNE alla caprese

Serves 4–6 • Preparation 10 minutes • Cooking 15 minutes Difficulty 1

1	pound (500 g) penne	2	cloves garlic, finely chopped
1 1/2	pounds (750 g) cherry tomatoes, halved	1/3	cup (90 ml) extra-virgin olive oil
8	ounces (250 g) mozzarella cheese, cut into small cubes		Salt and freshly ground black pepper
1/2	cup coarsely chopped fresh basil + extra, to garnish		

1. Cook the pasta in a large pot of salted boiling water until al dente, 10–12 minutes. Drain and toss with the tomatoes, mozzarella, basil, garlic, and oil in a large bowl. Season with salt and pepper.

2. Transfer to serving dishes and garnish with the extra basil. Serve hot.

TAGLIATELLE with almonds

Serves 4 • Preparation 15 minutes • Cooking 3–4 minutes Difficulty 1

14	ounces (400 g) fresh tagliatelle	3	tomatoes, peeled and chopped
1	cup (120 g) coarsely chopped almonds	1/2	teaspoon red pepper flakes
2	cloves garlic	1/2	cup (120 ml) extra-virgin olive oil
	Salt and freshly ground black pepper	4	tablespoons almond slivers, to garnish
1	large bunch fresh basil		

1. Chop the almonds, garlic, and a pinch of salt and pepper in a food processor until almost smooth. Add the basil and half the tomato and chop until smooth. Season with salt and red pepper flakes and stir in the oil.

2. Cook the pasta in a large pot of salted boiling water until al dente, 3–4 minutes.

3. Drain the pasta and place in a heated serving dish. Top with the sauce. Garnish with the remaining tomatoes, and sprinkle with the almond slivers. Serve hot.

HOT & SPICY spaghetti

Serves 4–6 • Preparation 15 minutes • Cooking 20–25 minutes • Difficulty 1

1/3	cup (90 g) extra-virgin olive oil	1	tablespoon tomato concentrate (purée)
4	cloves garlic, finely chopped	1	pound (500 g) spaghetti
2	red chilies, seeded and sliced		Freshly ground black pepper
2	pounds (1 kg) firm, ripe tomatoes, peeled and chopped	1/2	cup (60 g) Parmesan cheese, in flakes
1	cup (100 g) black olives, pitted	2	tablespoons fresh parsley, to garnish
2	tablespoons salt-cured capers, rinsed		

1. Heat the oil in a large frying pan over medium heat. Add the garlic and chilies and sauté until pale golden brown, 2–3 minutes. Add the tomatoes, olives, capers, and tomato concentrate and simmer over low heat for 15–20 minutes.

2. Cook the pasta in a large pot of salted boiling water until al dente, 10–12 minutes.

3. Drain the spaghetti and add to the pan with the sauce. Season with pepper. Toss over high heat for 1–2 minutes. Serve hot, garnished with the cheese and parsley.

This hearty dish is perfect for weeknight suppers during the cold winter months.

BAKED MACCHERONI with peas

Béchamel Sauce

3	tablespoons butter
3	tablespoons all-purpose (plain) flour
3	cups (750 ml) milk
	Salt and freshly ground black pepper
$1/2$	teaspoon freshly grated nutmeg
$1/4$	cup (30 g) dried porcini mushrooms, soaked in warm water for 15 minutes, drained (soaking liquid reserved), and finely chopped

Pasta

1	pound (500 g) maccheroni
5	tablespoons (75 g) butter
$1^1/4$	cups (150 g) freshly grated Parmesan cheese
7	ounces (200 g) mozzarella cheese, sliced
2	cups (300 g) frozen peas, thawed
$1/4$	cup (60 ml) milk
2	tablespoons fine dry bread crumbs

Serves 6 • Preparation 30 minutes + 10 minutes to rest • Cooking 40 minutes • Difficulty 1

Béchamel Sauce

1. Melt the butter in a medium saucepan over low heat. Add the flour and cook for 1–2 minutes, stirring constantly. Remove from the heat and add the milk all at once. Stir well then return to the heat. Season with the salt, pepper, and nutmeg. Bring to a boil and simmer, stirring constantly, until smooth and thick, about 5 minutes. Mix in the mushrooms with their soaking liquid and set aside.

Pasta

1. Cook the pasta in a large pot of salted boiling water for half the time indicated on the package. Drain and toss with 4 tablespoons of butter, 2 tablespoons of Parmesan, and one-third of the Béchamel.

2. Preheat the oven to 400°F (200°C/gas 6). Butter a large baking dish.

3. Spoon half the pasta into the prepared baking dish and sprinkle with half the remaining Parmesan. Top with the mozzarella and peas. Cover with half the remaining Béchamel. Spoon the remaining pasta into the dish, sprinkle with the remaining Parmesan, and pour the remaining Béchamel over the top. Drizzle with the milk, dot with the remaining butter, and sprinkle with the bread crumbs.

4. Bake for 15–20 minutes, until golden brown and bubbling. Remove from the oven and let rest for 10 minutes before serving.

TORTELLI with spinach & ricotta

Pasta
3	cups (450 g) all-purpose (plain) flour
4	large very fresh eggs, lightly beaten

Filling
1 1/2	pounds (750 g) tender spinach leaves, tough stalks removed
1/3	cup (90 g) butter
	Salt
	Pinch of nutmeg
8	ounces (250 g) fresh ricotta cheese, drained
1	cup (120 g) freshly grated Parmesan cheese

To Serve
1/2	cup (120 g) butter, melted
1	cup (120 g) freshly grated Parmesan cheese
2	tablespoons finely chopped fresh parsley, to garnish

Serves 4–6 • Preparation 45 minutes + 30 minutes to rest • Cooking 15 minutes • Difficulty 3

Pasta

1. Mound the flour up on a clean work surface. Make a well in the center and add the eggs. Use a fork to stir into the flour. Gather the dough up into a ball. Knead for 15 minutes. Wrap in plastic wrap (cling film). Let rest for 30 minutes.

Filling

1. Boil the spinach in salted boiling water until tender, 2–3 minutes. Drain well, and chop finely.

2. Melt the butter in a large frying pan. Add the spinach. Season with salt and nutmeg and sauté for 5 minutes. Let cool a little. Add the ricotta and Parmesan, mixing well.

3. Roll the pasta dough into paper thin sheets. Shape the filling into marble-size balls and place at regular intervals on half the sheets of pasta. Cover with the remaining sheets. Cut out the tortelli into squares or rounds using a fluted pasta cutter.

4. Bring a large pan of salted water to a boil. Cook the tortelli in batches until al dente, 3–4 minutes per batch. Remove with a slotted spoon and place in a heated serving dish.

5. Serve hot with the butter and freshly grated Parmesan cheese, garnished with parsley.

ORECCHIETTE with broccoli

1   medium head broccoli
¼   cup (60 ml) extra-virgin
     olive oil
3   cloves of garlic, finely
     chopped
1   red chili, seeded and thinly
     sliced
20   cherry tomatoes, halved
     Salt
1   pound (500 g) fresh
     orecchiette
1   cup (120 g) freshly grated
     pecorino or Parmesan cheese

Serves 4–6 • Preparation 30 minutes • Cooking 25–35 minutes
Difficulty 1

1. Trim the stem of the broccoli and dice into small cubes.
    Divide the broccoli heads into small florets. Boil the stem
    and florets in a large pot of salted water until tender, about
    8 minutes. Drain well, reserving the water to cook the pasta.

2. Heat the oil In a large frying pan over medium heat.
    Add the garlic and sauté until pale golden brown, 2–3
    minutes. Add the broccoli, chili, and cherry tomatoes,
    season with salt, and cook over low heat for 5 minutes.
    Remove from the heat.

3. Bring the water used to cook the broccoli back to a boil,
    add the pasta, and cook until al dente. Drain well, and add
    to the broccoli mixture in the pan.

4. Toss over high heat for 1–2 minutes. Remove from the heat,
    sprinkle with the cheese, and serve hot.

Paella is a traditional dish from the Mediterranean coast of southern Spain. It is made in a large, shallow pan in which the rice is left to cook over very low heat until tender and with a delicious crisp bottom.

68

VEGETARIAN paella

$1/3$	cup (90 ml) extra-virgin olive oil
2	small red onions, finely chopped
2	red bell peppers (capsicum), seeded and cut into strips
1	yellow bell pepper (capsicum), seeded and cut into strips
1	green bell pepper (capsicum), seeded and cut into strips
1	bulb fennel, trimmed and thinly sliced
2	cloves garlic, sliced
3	bay leaves
1	teaspoon smoked paprika
1	teaspoon turmeric
1	teaspoon cayenne
$1^1/2$	cups (300 g) calasparra rice
$3/4$	cup (180 ml) sherry
2	teaspoons saffron strands
4	cups (1 liter) boiling vegetable stock
	Salt
24	cherry tomatoes, halved
10	small grilled artichokes, from a jar, quartered
2	cups (300 g) frozen peas, thawed
16	pitted Kalamata olives
4	tablespoons coarsely chopped fresh parsley
8	lemon wedges, to serve

Serves 4-6 • Preparation 30 minutes + 10 minutes to rest • Cooking 25–30 minutes • Difficulty 2

1. Heat the oil in a large paella or frying pan over medium heat. Add the onion and sauté until softened, 3-4 minutes. Add the bell peppers and fennel, and sauté until softened, 8-10 minutes.

2. Add the garlic, cook for 1 minute, then add the bay leaves, paprika, turmeric, cayenne, and rice and cook, stirring, for 2 minutes. Add the sherry and saffron, boil down for 1-2 minutes, then add the vegetable stock and a generous pinch of salt. Reduce the heat to very low and leave to simmer until most of the liquid has been absorbed, about 20 minutes. Do not stir; the very low heat will stop the rice from sticking to the bottom of the pan, and a delicious crispy crust will form.

3. Remove the pan from the heat. Season with salt if needed, but do not the rice and vegetables much. Sprinkle the tomatoes, artichokes, and peas over the rice, cover the pan tightly with aluminum foil and set aside to rest for 10 minutes.

4. Remove the foil, sprinkle with the olives and parsley and serve hot with lemon wedges.

SPINACH risotto

1 pound (500 g) baby spinach leaves + a few extra, to garnish

8 tablespoons (120 g) butter

1/2 cup (60 g) freshly grated Parmesan cheese + extra flakes, to garnish

Salt and freshly ground black pepper

1 small white onion, finely chopped

1/2 cup (120 ml) dry white wine

2 cups (400 g) Italian risotto rice, such Arborio

6 cups (1.5 liters) boiling vegetable stock

Serves 4-6 • Preparation 25 minutes • Cooking 30–35 minutes
Difficulty 1

1. Cook the baby spinach leaves in a little salted water until just tender, 3–5 minutes. Drain well and chop finely.

2. Melt 6 tablespoons of the butter in a large saucepan over low heat. Add the spinach and Parmesan. Season with salt and pepper, stirring well. Set aside.

3. Heat the remaining 2 tablespoons of butter in a large frying pan over medium heat. Add the onion and sauté until softened, 3–4 minutes. Increase the heat to medium-high and add the rice. Stir constantly for 2–3 minutes. Add the wine and stir until evaporated. Begin adding the stock, 1/2 cup (120 ml) at a time, cooking and stirring until each addition has been absorbed and the rice is tender, about 20 minutes.

4. Stir in the spinach mixture, and serve hot, garnished with the extra spinach leaves and the flakes of Parmesan.

ASPARAGUS risotto

4 tablespoons (60 g) butter

1 1/2 pounds (750 g) asparagus, trimmed, stalks chopped and tips reserved

6 cups (1.5 liters) boiling vegetable stock

1 onion, finely chopped

2 cups (400 g) Italian risotto rice, such as Arborio

1/3 cup (90 ml) dry white wine

1/4 cup (60 ml) heavy (double) cream, boiling

1/2 cup (60 g) freshly grated Parmesan cheese

Freshly ground white pepper

Coarsely chopped fresh parsley, to garnish

Serves 4–6 • Preparation 30 minutes • Cooking 35–40 minutes
Difficulty 1

1. Heat 2 tablespoons of butter in a large frying pan over low heat. Add the chopped asparagus stalks and sauté for 2–3 minutes. Pour in 1 cup (250 ml) of stock and bring to a boil. Simmer until the asparagus is very tender, about 10 minutes. Transfer to a food processor and chop until smooth. Set aside in a bowl.

2. Heat the remaining butter in a large saucepan over low heat. Add the onion and sauté until softened, 3–4 minutes. Stir in the rice. Cook for 2 minutes, stirring constantly. Stir in the wine, and when this has been absorbed, begin stirring in the stock, 1/2 cup (120 ml) at a time. After about 10 minutes, add the asparagus purée and the tips. Keep adding stock, cooking and stirring until each addition has been absorbed, until the rice is tender, about 20 minutes.

3. Add the cream and Parmesan, and season with pepper. Serve hot garnished with the parsley.

Risotto is a traditional northern Italian dish. It is made with special plump, short-grain types of rice such as Arborio, which release their starches gradually during the slow cooking and stirring process, so that the finished dish is smooth and creamy.

BLUE CHEESE RISOTTO with pears

1/3   cup (90 g) butter
1   small onion, finely chopped
2   cups (400 g) Italian risotto rice, such as Arborio
2   firm-ripe pears, finely chopped
1/2   cup (120 ml) brandy
6   cups (1.5 liters) boiling vegetable stock
8   ounces (250 g) blue cheese, such as Gorgonzola, Roquefort, or Stilton
1/2   cup (60 g) coarsely chopped walnuts, to garnish
2   tablespoons finely chopped fresh parsley, to garnish

Serves 4–6 • Preparation 20 minutes • Cooking 25–30 minutes
Difficulty 1

1. Heat the butter in a large frying pan over medium heat. add the onion and sauté until softened, 3–4 minutes. Stir in the rice and pears and cook for 2 minutes. Pour in the brandy and cook until the brandy has evaporated.

2. Add 1/2 cup (120 ml) of stock and stir until absorbed. Keep adding stock, 1/2 cup (120 ml) at a time, cooking and stirring until each addition has been absorbed and the rice is tender and creamy, about 20 minutes. Add the cheese and remove from the heat.

3. Dry-fry the walnuts in a frying pan over medium heat until crisp and golden.

4. Ladle the risotto into serving dishes and garnish with the walnuts and parsley. Serve hot.

If you liked this recipe, you will love these as well.

SPINACH risotto

ASPARAGUS risotto

PEARL BARLEY risotto

BROWN RICE with edamame

$^3/_4$ cup (150 g) long-grain brown rice

$1^1/_4$ cups (200 g) frozen shelled edamame (green, baby soy beans)

1 tablespoon freshly squeezed lime juice

1 tablespoon rice vinegar

$1^1/_2$ teaspoons sesame oil

$^1/_2$ teaspoon brown sugar

3 scallions (spring onions), trimmed and thinly sliced on the diagonal

Salt and freshly ground black pepper

Serves 4–6 • Preparation 25 minutes • Cooking 45–50 minutes
Difficulty 1

1. Bring $1^1/_2$ cups (375 ml) of lightly salted water to a boil in a medium saucepan. Add the rice and return to a boil. Reduce the heat, cover, and simmer for 30 minutes.

2. Stir in the edamame, cover, and simmer until the rice is tender, 15–20 minutes.

3. Whisk the lime juice, vinegar, oil, and sugar in a small bowl until well combined and the sugar is dissolved.

4. Stir the lime juice mixture and scallions into the rice. Season with salt and pepper, and serve hot.

PEARL BARLEY risotto

3 tablespoons extra-virgin olive oil

1½ cups (270 g) pearl barley

3 leeks, white and light green parts only, thinly sliced

½ cup (120 ml) dry white wine

2 cups (500 ml) water

Salt and freshly ground black pepper

3 cups (750 ml) vegetable stock

1 pound (500 g) asparagus, trimmed and cut into short pieces

2 cups (300 g) frozen peas

½ cup (60 g) freshly grated Parmesan cheese

¼ cup finely chopped fresh mint + extra leaves, to garnish

Serves 4–6 • Preparation 30 minutes • Cooking 35–40 minutes
Difficulty 2

1. Heat the oil in a large frying pan over medium heat. Add the barley and leeks and stir until starting to soften, 5–7 minutes. Add the wine and stir until evaporated, about 5 minutes. Add the water, bring to a boil, and season with salt and pepper. Reduce the heat and simmer until the liquid has been absorbed, about 10 minutes.

2. Add the vegetable stock and continue to cook, stirring occasionally, until the barley is almost tender and creamy, about 10 minutes. Add the asparagus and peas and cook until tender, about 5 minutes.

3. Stir in the Parmesan and mint. Season with salt and pepper. Garnish with extra mint leaves, and serve hot.

Pearl barely is a good source of dietary fiber and manganese. It is very low in saturated fat, cholesterol, and sodium, making it a healthy food choice. Cooking time varies from 20–30 minutes. There are some precooked types available now that are ready in 10 minutes.

PEARL BARLEY with sundried tomato pesto

1½ cups (300 g) pearl barley

½ cup (75 g) blanched almonds, toasted

12 sundried tomatoes in oil, drained

1 tablespoon salt-cured capers, rinsed

⅓ cup (90 ml) extra-virgin olive oil

Freshly squeezed juice of ½ lemon

8 ounces (250 g) fresh mozzarella, cut into small cubes

2 cups (100 g) arugula (rocket)

½ cup (50 g) Parmesan cheese, in flakes

Serves 4-6 • Preparation 10 minutes • Cooking 20–30 minutes
Difficulty 1

1. Cook the pearl barley in a large pot of salted, boiling water until tender, 20–30 minutes. Drain well.

2. Put the almonds, sundried tomatoes, capers, oil, and lemon juice in a food processor and chop until smooth.

3. Stir the sundried tomato pesto and mozzarella into the hot pearl barley. The mozzarella will begin to melt.

4. Arrange the arugula in four to six serving dishes. Top with the pearly barley mixture and sprinkle with the Parmesan. Serve hot.

If you liked this recipe, you will love these as well.

SPINACH risotto

BROWN RICE
with edamame

PEARL BARLEY
risotto

veggies & beans

BEAN & BULGUR burgers

Burgers

$\frac{1}{2}$	cup (90 g) medium-grind bulgur
	Salt and freshly ground black pepper
1	cup (250 ml) boiling water
4	tablespoons (60 ml) extra-virgin olive oil
1	onion, finely chopped
1	clove garlic, finely chopped
1	teaspoon ground cumin
$\frac{1}{2}$	teaspoon ground coriander
2	(14-ounce/400-g) cans red kidney beans, rinsed and drained
$\frac{1}{2}$	cup (50 g) finely ground almonds

To Serve

4	whole-wheat (wholemeal) or granary burger buns, halved and toasted
	Lettuce leaves
	Sliced tomatoes
	Natural yogurt
	Ketchup

Serves 4 • Preparation 30 minutes + 1 hour to soak and chill • Cooking 15–20 minutes • Difficulty 2

Burgers

1. Mix the bulgur with $\frac{1}{4}$ teaspoon of salt and the boiling water. Cover and set aside until tender, about 30 minutes. Drain, squeezing out excess moisture.

2. Heat 2 tablespoons of the oil in a large frying pan over medium heat. Add the onion and garlic and sauté until softened, 3–4 minutes. Stir in the cumin and coriander and simmer for 1 minute. Set aside to cool.

3. Put the kidney beans in a bowl and mash with a fork. Stir in the onion mixture, bulgur, and almonds. Season wiuth salt and pepper and shape into burgers. Chill for 30 minutes.

4. Heat the remaining oil in a large frying pan over medium heat. Cook the burgers until golden, 5–6 minutes each side.

To Serve

1. Fill the rolls with the lettuce, tomatoes, and burgers. Add a dollop each of yogurt and ketchup, and serve hot.

If you liked this recipe, you will love these as well.

VEGGIE burgers

SPICY BEAN burgers

TUSCAN CANNELLINI BEAN stew

VEGGIE burgers

Burgers

1/2	cup (90 g) medium-grind bulgar
	Salt and freshly ground black pepper
1	cup (250 ml) boiling water
2	(14-ounce/400-g) cans pinto beans, rinsed and drained
1/4	cup (30 g) fine dry bread crumbs
4	scallions (spring onions), thinly sliced
1	large egg
1	large carrot, coarsely grated
1/4	teaspoon cayenne pepper
2	tablespoons tahini
3	tablespoons vegetable oil

To Serve

4	hamburger buns, halved and toasted
	Lettuce
	Sweet chili sauce

Serves 4 • Preparation 15 minutes + 30 minutes to soak • Cooking 10–12 minutes • Difficulty 1

Burgers

1. Mix the bulgur with 1/4 teaspoon of salt and the boiling water. Cover and set aside until tender, about 30 minutes. Drain, squeezing out excess moisture.

2. Put the beans in a bowl and mash with a fork until smooth. Add the bread crumbs, scallions, egg, carrot, cayenne, tahini, and bulgur. Season with salt and pepper, mixing well. Form into four burgers.

3. Heat the oil in a large frying pan over medium-high heat. Cook the burgers until golden, 5–6 minutes each side.

To Serve

1. Fill the rolls with the lettuce and burgers and spread with sweet chili sauce. Serve hot

SPICY BEAN burgers

Salsa

3	ripe tomatoes, diced
1	clove garlic, finely chopped
1	small onion, finely chopped
1/4	fresh red chili, seeded and finely chopped
1	tablespoon finely chopped fresh cilantro (coriander)

Burgers

2	(14-ounce/400-g) cans cannellini or white kidney beans, rinsed and drained
2/3	cup (100 g) fine dry bread crumbs
2	teaspoons chile powder
4	tablespoons coarsely chopped fresh cilantro (coriander)
1	large egg
	Salt and freshly ground black pepper
2/3	cup (150 ml) plain yogurt
	Freshly squeezed juice of 1/2 lime
4	whole-wheat (wholemeal) burger buns
1	avocado, pitted and sliced
1	small red onion, sliced
	Salad leaves, to serve

Serves 4 • Preparation 20 minutes + 30 minutes to rest • Cooking 8–10 minutes • Difficulty 1

Salsa

1. Mix the tomatoes, garlic, onion, chili, and cilantro in a bowl and let rest for 30 minutes at room temperature.

Burgers

1. Coarsely mash the beans in a large bowl. Add the bread crumbs, chile powder, 3 tablespoons of cilantro, the egg, and 2 tablespoons of salsa. Season with salt and pepper. Divide the mixture into four and form into burgers.

2. Heat a grill pan (griddle) on high heat. Grill the burgers until golden and crisp, 4–5 minutes on each side.

3. Mix the remaining cilantro with the yogurt, lime juice, and black pepper. Split the buns in half and spread with some of the yogurt mixture. Top with salad, avocado, onion, a burger, more yogurt, and some salsa. Serve hot.

This is a rich and nourishing curry that can be served with rice as a meal in itself. Feel free to vary the vegetables according to what is in season, what you like, and what you have on hand.

VEGGIE & COCONUT curry

Spice Paste

4-6	dried red chilies, crumbled
1	teaspoon coriander seeds
2	cloves garlic, finely chopped
6	shallots, chopped
1	teaspoon ground turmeric
1	tablespoon finely grated ginger

Curry

4	tablespoons (60 ml) peanut oil
3	cups (750 ml) coconut milk
1	cup fresh pineapple, cubed
1	cup (150 g) frozen peas
5	ounces (150 g) white mushrooms, sliced
2	pak choy, coarsely chopped
2	tomatoes, sliced
2	star anise, chopped
1	stick cinnamon
$1/4$	teaspoon ground cloves
$1/8$	teaspoon ground nutmeg
1	stalk lemongrass, finely chopped
1	tablespoon freshly squeezed lime juice
	Salt and freshly ground black pepper
2	shallots, sliced
	Fresh cilantro (coriander), to garnish
	Freshly cooked basmati rice, to serve

Serves 4–6 • Preparation 20 minutes • Cooking 15–20 minutes Difficulty 2

Spice Paste

1. Grind the chilies, coriander seeds, garlic, shallots, turmeric, and ginger with a pestle and mortar until crushed.

Curry

1. Heat 2 tablespoons of the oil in a large wok or frying pan and sauté the spice paste until aromatic. Pour in the coconut milk and bring to a boil, stirring constantly.

2. Add the pineapple, peas, mushrooms, pak choy, tomatoes, star anise, cinnamon, cloves, nutmeg, lemongrass, and lime juice. Season with salt and pepper. Cook over medium heat until the vegetables are tender, 10–15 minutes.

3. Heat the remaining oil in a small frying pan over medium-high heat. Fry the shallots until crisp and browned. Garnish the curry with the fried shallots and cilantro and serve hot with the rice.

If you liked this recipe, you will love these as well.

TOFU & VEGGIE curry

SPICY TOFU stir-fry

MEDITERRANEAN VEGGIE stew

TOFU & VEGGIE curry

2   tablespoons peanut oil
2   onions, diced
5   cloves garlic, finely chopped
14   ounces (400 g) firm tofu,
       cut into small cubes
1   teaspoon garam masala
$\frac{1}{2}$ teaspoon turmeric
$\frac{1}{2}$ teaspoon ground cumin
4   tomatoes, diced
       Salt and freshly ground black
       pepper
4   cups (200 g) fresh spinach

Serves 4 • Preparation 10 minutes • Cooking 15 minutes • Difficulty 1

1. Heat the oil in a large frying pan over medium heat. Add the onions and garlic and sauté until softened, 3-4 minutes.

2. Add the tofu, garam masala, turmeric, cumin, and tomatoes. Season with salt and pepper and cook, stirring frequently, for about 5 minutes, until the tofu is hot.

3. Add the spinach and cook, stirring well, until wilted, 1-2 minutes. Serve hot.

SPICY TOFU *stir-fry*

Spice Paste

1	ounce (30 g) fresh ginger, peeled
2	lemongrass stalks
2	red chilies
3	shallots, chopped
1	clove garlic
1	teaspoon turmeric
1/4	teaspoon salt
2	tablespoons peanut oil

Sauce

| 1 | (14-ounce/400-ml) can coconut milk |
| 1 | cup (250 ml) vegetable stock |

Curry

	Vegetable oil, for deep-frying + 1 tablespoon, for frying
8	ounces (250 g) firm tofu, cut into 1-inch (2.5-cm) cubes
20	oyster mushrooms, sliced
12	sugar snap peas (mangetout), halved
14	ounces (400 g) udon noodles, cooked according to the instructions on the package
	Fresh cilantro (coriander), to serve
	Lime wedges, to serve
	Coarsely chopped peanuts, to serve

Spice Paste

1. Place all the spice paste ingredients, except the peanut oil, in a food processor and blend to a pulp. With the motor still running, gradually add the oil and blend to a paste.

Sauce

1. Place a frying pan over medium heat. Sauté the spice paste for 2–3 minutes. Add the coconut milk and vegetable stock and bring to a boil. Simmer for 5 minutes.

Curry

1. Half-fill a deep, heavy-based pan with vegetable oil and place over medium heat. Test by dropping in a small piece of bread. If it immediately turns golden and bubbles to the surface, the oil is ready. Add the tofu and deep-fry until crisp and golden-brown, 2–3 minutes. Remove with a slotted spoon and drain on paper towels.

2. Heat the remaining 1 tablespoon of oil in a frying pan over medium heat. Add the mushrooms and sauté until softened, 3–4 minutes. Add the mushrooms to the sauce. Add the sugar snap peas, tofu, and noodles to the sauce.

3. Garnish with fresh cilantro, lime wedges, and peanuts and serve hot.

These crêpes are a special treat. You can prepare them from late spring to high summer when zucchini flowers (courgette blossoms) are available from farmers' markets. The flowers are so pretty you may want to reserve a couple and use them to garnish the finished dish.

RICOTTA & ZUCCHINI crêpes

Crêpes

1²/₃ cups (250 g) all-purpose (plain) flour

2 cups (500 ml) milk

4 large eggs

1 tablespoon finely chopped fresh thyme

1 tablespoon finely chopped fresh marjoram

1 tablespoon finely chopped fresh parsley

¹/₂ teaspoon salt

1 tablespoon butter

Ricotta Filling

12 ounces (350 g) zucchini (courgettes), cut into rounds

2 tablespoons butter

24 zucchini flowers (courgette blossoms)

14 ounces (400 g) ricotta cheese

¹/₂ cup (60 g) pine nuts, toasted

¹/₂ teaspoon freshly ground nutmeg

1¹/₄ cups (300 ml) heavy (double) cream

1 tablespoon freshly grated Parmesan cheese

Serves 6 • Preparation 45 minutes • Cooking 30 minutes • Difficulty 3

Crêpes

1. Mix the flour and milk in a large bowl. Add the eggs and beat until well blended. Beat in the thyme, marjoram, and parsley. Season with salt.

2. Melt the butter in a small frying pan over medium heat. Pour in just enough batter to cover the bottom of the pan, tilting it so that it thinly covers the surface. Cook until the crêpe is lightly gold on the underside. Use a large spatula to flip and cook the other side. Repeat until all the batter has been used. Stack the cooked crêpes one on top of another in a warm oven.

3. Preheat the oven to 400°F (200°C/gas 6). Butter a large baking dish.

Ricotta Filling

1. Sauté the zucchini in the butter in a large frying pan over medium heat until softened, 5–10 minutes. Add the zucchini flowers, ricotta, pine nuts, and nutmeg. Cook for 3 minutes.

2. Place 2–3 tablespoons of filling in the center of each crêpe. Fold the crêpes in half and then in half again to form triangles.

3. Arrange the filled crêpes in the prepared baking dish. Pour the cream over the top and sprinkle with the Parmesan.

4. Cover with aluminum foil and bake for 10 minutes. Remove the foil and bake for 8–10 minutes more, until the crêpes are crisp and the cheese is golden brown. Serve hot.

ASPARAGUS & ALMOND loaf

1	pound (500 g) asparagus stalks, trimmed
1	zucchini (courgette), thinly sliced
6	tablespoons freshly grated Parmesan cheese
	Salt and freshly ground black pepper
2	tablespoons butter, melted
6	large eggs
$2/3$	cup (150 ml) heavy (double) cream
2	tablespoons slivered almonds
	Salad greens, to serve

Serves 4 • Preparation 20 minutes • Cooking 15–20 minutes • Difficulty 1

1. Preheat the oven to 400°F (200°C/gas 6). Butter a large rectangular loaf pan.

2. Cook the asparagus in a large pot of salted boiling water until almost tender, 3–5 minutes. Drain and chop coarsely.

3. Arrange the asparagus and zucchini in layers in the prepared loaf pan. Sprinkle each layer with Parmesan and season with salt and pepper. Drizzle with the melted butter. Beat the eggs and cream in a bowl until well blended. Pour the mixture over the vegetables. Sprinkle with the almonds.

4. Bake for 10–15 minutes, until firm and golden. Slice and serve hot or at room temperature with the salad greens.

ASPARAGUS & OLIVE loaf

Serves 4 • Preparation 20 minutes • Cooking 40–45 minutes • Difficulty 1

8 ounces (250 g) asparagus stalks
1⅓ cups (200 g) self-rising flour
1 tablespoon fresh thyme leaves
Salt and freshly ground black pepper
3 large eggs, lightly beaten
½ cup (120 ml) milk
⅓ cup (90 ml) extra-virgin olive oil
1 cup (100 g) sundried tomatoes, coarsely chopped
½ cup (50 g) pitted black olives
1 cup (140 g) freshly grated Gruyère cheese

1. Preheat the oven to 375°F (190°C/gas 5). Butter a large rectangular loaf pan.

2. Cook the asparagus in a large pot of salted boiling water until almost tender, 3–5 minutes. Drain and chop coarsely.

3. Mix the flour and thyme in a large bowl. Season with salt and pepper. Make a well in the center and stir in the eggs, milk, and oil.

4. Add the sparagus, sundried tomatoes, olives, and two-thirds of the cheese to the batter. Pour into the prepared pan. Sprinkle with the remaining cheese.

5. Bake for 35–40 minutes, until firm and golden. Slice and serve hot or at room temperature.

EGGPLANT stew

Serves 6-8 • Preparation 30 minutes • Cooking 35-40 minutes • Difficulty 2

¼	cup (60 ml) extra-virgin olive oil	1	bay leaf
3	pounds (1.5 kg) eggplant (aubergines), cut into small cubes	1	teaspoon sugar
		8	cloves garlic, finely chopped
2	pounds (1 kg) tomatoes, peeled, seeded, and finely chopped	½	cup (120 ml) milk
			Salt and freshly ground black pepper

1. Heat the oil in a large frying pan over medium heat. Sauté the eggplants until tender. Drain well, reserving the oil. Set aside.

2. Reheat the oil in a saucepan over medium heat. Add the tomatoes and bay leaf and cook until softened. Stir in the sugar and garlic. Simmer for 5-8 minutes. Remove from the heat and pour in the milk. Season with salt.

3. Chop the cooked eggplants in a food processor. Stir into the tomato mixture. Season with pepper. Cook over low heat for 15-20 minutes, until well blended. Serve hot.

CAPONATA with rice

Serves 4 • Preparation 25 minutes • Cooking 25-30 minutes • Difficulty 2

2	eggplant (aubergines), diced	1	tablespoon salt-cured capers, rinsed of salt
1	small onion, chopped	1	tablespoon sugar
3	tablespoons extra-virgin olive oil		Salt and freshly ground black pepper
2	stalks celery, chopped	4	tablespoons water
4	tomatoes, chopped	2	tablespoons vinegar
1	pear, peeled and coarsely chopped	1½	cups (300 g) rice
1	cup (100 g) black olives	1	tablespoon finely chopped fresh basil

1. Sauté the eggplants and onion in 1 tablespoon of oil in a large frying pan over medium heat until softened, 8-10 minutes. Add the celery, tomatoes, pear, olives, capers, sugar, salt, and pepper. Add the water and vinegar. Simmer until tender, 15 minutes.

2. Cook the rice in a large pot of salted boiling water for 12-15 minutes, or until tender. Drain and drizzle with the remaining oil. Stir in the basil.

3. Fill four small molds with the rice, pressing down firmly. Turn out onto serving plates and serve with the caponata.

BLACK BEAN chili

Serves 6 • Preparation 20 minutes • Cooking 25-30 minutes • Difficulty 1

1	tablespoon extra-virgin olive oil		black beans, rinsed and drained
1	small onion, diced	1	cup (250 ml) water
2	garlic cloves, minced	2	(14-ounce/400-g) cans crushed tomatoes
	Salt and freshly ground black pepper	2	cups (300 g) frozen corn (sweetcorn) kernels
2	zucchini, thinly sliced		
2	carrots, thinly sliced		Fresh cilantro (coriander), to garnish
1	tablespoon chile powder		Sour cream, to serve
1	teaspoon ground cumin		
2	(14-ounce/400-g) cans		

1. Heat the oil in a heavy pot over medium-high heat. Add the onion and garlic and sauté until softened, 3-4 minutes. Season with salt and pepper.

2. Add the zucchini, carrots, chile powder, and cumin. Cook, stirring occasionally, for 10 minutes.

3. Add the beans, tomatoes, corn, and water. Simmer until slightly thickened and the carrots are soft, 8-10 minutes more.

4. Serve hot, garnished with the cilantro and sour cream.

CAULIFLOWER stew

Serves 4 • Preparation 25 minutes • Cooking 30 minutes Difficulty 1

¼	cup (60 ml) extra-virgin olive oil	2	pounds (1 kg) tomatoes, peeled and chopped
4	cloves garlic, finely chopped	1	medium cauliflower, cut into florets
1	teaspoon fennel seeds		Salt and freshly ground black pepper
2	tablespoons finely chopped fresh parsley		

1. Heat the oil in a large frying pan over medium-high heat. Add the garlic, fennel seeds, and parsley and sauté until the garlic is pale gold, 3-4 minutes. Stir in the tomatoes and simmer for 15 minutes.

2. Add the cauliflower to the tomato sauce and season with salt and pepper. Cover and simmer over low heat until the cauliflower is tender, about 10 minutes. Serve hot.

MEDITERRANEAN VEGGIE stew

¹/₄	cup (60 ml) extra-virgin olive oil
2	medium potatoes, peeled and cut into small cubes
1	large onion, finely chopped
1	red bell pepper (capsicum), seeded and cut into small chunks
1	green bell pepper (capsicum), seeded and cut into small chunks
1	eggplant (aubergine), cut into small cubes
1	large zucchini (courgette), cut into small cubes
2	pounds (1 kg) tomatoes, coarsely chopped
	Salt and freshly ground black pepper
¹/₄	cup (60 ml) water, if needed
	Freshly prepared couscous, to serve
	Fresh basil, to garnish

Serves 4 • Preparation 20 minutes • Cooking 25–30 minutes • Difficulty 1

1. Heat the oil in a large frying pan over medium heat. Add the potatoes and sauté until golden, 4–5 minutes. Add the onion and bell peppers and cook, stirring often, until the onion is lightly browned, about 5 minutes. Add the eggplant and zucchini and cook for 5 minutes.

2. Stir in the tomatoes. Season with salt and pepper. Cook for until the vegetables are tender, adding the water if the mixture begins to stick to the pan.

3. Serve hot with the couscous, garnished with basil.

TUSCAN CANNELLINI bean stew

2 pounds (1 kg) ripe tomatoes

2 cups (300 g) dried cannellini beans, soaked overnight and drained

6 cloves garlic, lightly crushed but whole

1 bay leaf

1–2 fresh or dried chilies

4 cups (1 liter) water

Salt and freshly ground black pepper

Fresh basil, to garnish

¼ cup (60 ml) extra-virgin olive oil

Serves 4–6 • Preparation 20 minutes + 12 hours to soak the beans
Cooking 1 hour • Difficulty 1

1. Blanch the tomatoes in salted boiling water for 1 minute. Drain and slip off the skins. Remove the seeds and chop the flesh coarsely.

2. Place the beans in a large pan with the tomatoes, garlic, bay leaf, and chilies. Pour in enough water to cover the beans completely and bring to a boil. Cover and simmer over low heat until the beans are tender, about 1 hour. Season with salt halfway through the cooking.

3. Discard the garlic and bay leaf. Garnish with the basil, season with pepper, and drizzle with the oil. Serve hot.

These tomatoes are a tasty treat. Be sure to choose eight unblemished tomatoes, all of about the same size. They will serve four as a main and eight as an appetizer.

BAKED RISOTTO tomatoes

8	medium tomatoes
5	tablespoons (75 g) butter
1	tablespoon very finely chopped onion
1	cup (200 g) Italian risotto rice, such as Arborio
2	cups (500 ml) boiling vegetable stock
1/2	cup (60 g) freshly grated Parmesan cheese
	Salt and freshly ground black pepper
2	large eggs
2	cups (300 g) fine dry bread crumbs

Serves 4–8 • Preparation 30 minutes • Cooking 1 hour • Difficulty 3

1. Preheat the oven to 400°F (200°C/gas 6). Butter a shallow ovenproof dish into which the tomatoes will fit snugly.

2. Rinse and dry the tomatoes and cut a 1/2-inch (1-cm) thick slice from the stalk end. Set these "lids" aside. Discard the flesh and seeds.

3. Melt 2 tablespoons of the butter in a large frying pan over medium heat. add the onion and sauté until transparent, 2–3 minutes. Add the rice and cook for 2 minutes, stirring constantly.

4. Begin stirring in the stock, 1/2 cup (120 ml) at a time. Cook and stir until each addition has been absorbed, until the rice is tender, about 20 minutes. Stir in the Parmesan and season with salt and pepper.

5. Stuff the tomatoes with the risotto and top each one neatly with its lid. Beat the eggs lightly in a bowl and dip the bottoms of the stuffed tomatoes into the beaten egg. Coat with the bread crumbs.

6. Place the tomatoes in a single layer, lid-side uppermost, in the prepared baking dish. Top each one with a flake of the remaining butter.

7. Bake for 25–30 minutes, until tender and golden. Serve hot or at room temperature.

VEGETARIAN shepherd's pie

2	tablespoons extra-virgin olive oil
2	onions, sliced
3	carrots, cut into small cubes
2	tablespoons fresh thyme chopped
3/4	cup (200 ml) red wine
2/3	cup (150 ml) water
1	(14-ounce/400-g) can tomatoes, drained
2	vegetable stock cubes, crumbled
1	(14-ounce/400-g) can garbanzo beans (chickpeas), drained and coarsely mashed with a fork
2	pounds (1 kg) sweet potatoes, peeled and cut into chunks
2	tablespoons butter
	Salt and freshly ground black pepper
3/4	cup (80 g) freshly grated Cheddar cheese

Serves 4 • Preparation 30 minutes • Cooking 45–50 minutes • Difficulty 1

1. Preheat the oven to 375°F (190°C/gas 5).

2. Heat the oil in a large frying pan over medium heat. Add the onion and sauté until golden. Add the carrots and almost all the thyme. Pour in the wine, water, tomatoes, and stock cubes and simmer for 10 minutes. Add the garbanzo beans. Cover and simmer for 10 more minutes.

3. Boil the sweet potatoes until tender, about 15 minutes. Drain well, and mash with the butter. Season with salt and pepper. Pile the bean mixture into a pie dish, spoon the sweet potato mash on top, and sprinkle with the cheese and remaining thyme.

4. Bake for 20 minutes, until the topping is golden and bubbling. Let rest for 5 minutes before serving.

VEGETARIAN lasagna

4   pounds (2 kg) spinach, steamed and chopped
$^3/_4$ cup (180 g) unsalted butter
3   cloves garlic, thinly sliced
1   pound (500 g) ricotta cheese
     Salt and freshly ground black pepper
2   pounds (1 kg) mixed wild mushrooms , trimmed, cut into small pieces
$^2/_3$ cup (180 ml) sherry
$^1/_2$ cup chopped fresh parsley
4   cups (1 liter) milk
$^1/_2$ cup (75 g) all-purpose (plain) flour
$^1/_2$ teaspoon ground nutmeg
1   cup (120 g) freshly grated Parmesan cheese
1   (1-pound/500-g) package fresh lasagna sheets

Serves 8–10 • Preparation 45 minutes + 15 minutes to stand • Cooking 1½ hours • Difficulty 2

1. Melt 3 tablespoons of butter in large frying pan over medium heat. Add the garlic and saute until golden, 2–3 minutes. Add the spinach and cook until well mixed. Place in a bowl with the ricotta. Season with salt and pepper.

2. Melt 6 tablespoons of butter in a large frying pan over medium heat. Add the mushrooms, season with salt and pepper, and saute until softened. Add the sherry and cook until evaporated. Transfer to a bowl. Add the parsley.

3. Heat the milk in a saucepan. Melt 8 tablespoons butter in a saucepan over medium heat. Add the flour and cook, stirring constantly, for 1 minute. Slowly add the milk, stirring constantly, until thick. Remove from the heat. Season with salt, pepper, nutmeg, and half the cheese.

4. Preheat the oven to 350°F (180°C/gas 4). Spread ½ cup of sauce in a large baking pan. Cover with lasagna sheets, trimming to fit. Spread with 1 cup of spinach mixture, 1 cup of mushroom mixture, and ½ cup of sauce. Repeat, finishing with a layer of lasagna, spread with sauce and the remaining cheese. Bake for about 1 hour, until top golden brown. Let stand for 15 minutes before serving.

ZUCCHINI frittata

Serves 4 • Preparation 20 minutes • Cooking 30 minutes • Difficulty 1

4	tablespoons butter		Salt and freshly ground black pepper
12	ounces (350 g) white mushrooms	8	eggs, lightly beaten
2	cloves garlic, lightly crushed but whole	1/3	cup (40 g) freshly grated Parmesan
2	zucchini (courgettes), thinly sliced	3	tablespoons milk
1	sprig thyme, finely chopped	2	tablespoons sesame seeds

1. Heat 2 tablespoons of butter in a large frying pan over medium heat. Add the mushrooms and sauté until tender, about 10 minutes.

2. Discard the garlic and add the zucchini and thyme. Season with salt and pepper. Cook for 10 minutes.

3. Put the eggs in a large. Stir in the Parmesan and milk. Season with salt and pepper. Pour over the mushrooms and zucchini and cook until set, 4–5 minutes. Sprinkle with the sesame seeds.

4. Turn the frittata and cook for 4 minutes. It should be firm and lightly browned on both sides. Serve hot.

SWEET POTATO bake

Serves 4 • Preparation 25 minutes • Cooking 30 minutes Difficulty 1

2	pounds (1 kg) sweet potatoes, peeled and cut into cubes	2	tablespoons chopped fresh sage
1	pound (500 g) potatoes, peeled and cut into small cubes	1 1/2	cups (370 ml) milk, warmed
			Salt and freshly ground black pepper
1/2	cup (120 g) unsalted butter + 2 tablespoons, melted	3	slices white bread, crusts removed, crumbled

1. Simmer both potatoes in salted boiling water until tender, about 10 minutes. Drain and mash.

2. Preheat the oven to 375°F (190°C/gas 5). Melt 1/2 cup (120 g) butter in a small saucepan over medium heat, until golden brown, 5–7 minutes. Remove from the heat and add the sage. Stir the butter mixture and milk into the potatoes. Season with salt and pepper. Transfer to a casserole dish.

3. Combine the bread crumbs with 2 tablespoons melted butter and remaining 1/2 tablespoon of sage. Season with salt and pepper. Toss to combine.

4. Top the potato mixture with bread crumbs. Bake, uncovered, for 30–40 minutes, until bubbling and golden brown. Let stand for 10 minutes. Serve hot.

STUFFED bell peppers

Serves 6 • Preparation 30 minutes • Cooking 55–60 minutes • Difficulty 2

2	onions, chopped	2	tablespoons finely chopped fresh dill + extra, to garnish
4	tablespoons butter		
1	cup (200 g) rice	6	bell peppers (capsicums), tops cut off and seeded
2	tablespoons pumpkin and sunflower seeds		
2	tablespoons raisins	1	tablespoon tomato sauce
1	cup (250 ml) water		
	Salt and freshly ground black pepper	1	tablespoon paprika
3	tablespoons finely chopped fresh parsley	1	cup (250 ml) vegetable stock

1. Sauté the onions in the butter in a saucepan over low heat until golden, 10–15 minutes. Add the rice, pumpkin and sunflower seeds, raisins, and water and bring to a boil. Simmer until the rice is almost cooked, about 10 minutes. Season with salt and pepper. Add the parsley and dill. Set aside.

2. Preheat the oven to 350°F (180°C/gas 4). Oil a large baking dish. Spoon the filling into the bell peppers. Transfer to the baking dish. Mix the tomato sauce and paprika. Stir into the stock. Spoon over the bell peppers. Bake for 30 minutes. Serve hot with the dill.

SPICY VEGGIE bake

Serves 4 • Preparation 25 minutes • Cooking 30 minutes Difficulty 1

4	tablespoons (60 g) butter	2	cups (500 ml) water
1	cup (180 g) millet	2	large carrots, diced
1	onion, chopped	8	ounces (250 g) small potatoes, quartered
2	cups (100 g) shredded green cabbage	1/3	cup red lentils
2	cloves garlic, minced	1/2	cup canned garbanzo bean (chickpeas)
1	tablespoon freshly grated ginger	8	ounces (250 g) broccoli, chopped
1	tablespoon curry powder		Salt and freshly ground black pepper

1. Preheat the oven to 350°F (180°C/gas 4). Oil a large baking dish. Melt 1 tablespoon of butter in a large pan over medium heat. Add the millet and onion and sauté until softened, 3–4 minutes. Add the cabbage and sauté for 2–3 minutes. Add the garlic, ginger, and curry and simmer 2 minutes.

2. Add the water, carrots, potatoes, lentils, and garbanzos and bring to a boil. Cover and simmer for 20 minutes. Stir in the broccoli. Season with salt and pepper.

3. Transfer to the baking dish and cover with millet mixture. Dot with the remaining butter. Bake for 30 minutes, until golden brown. Serve hot.

vegetarian

100

GREEN BEAN casserole

6   tablespoons (90 g) unsalted butter
1   medium onion, cut into small dice
1   red bell pepper (capsicum), seeded and cut into small dice
1   pound (500 g) button mushrooms, stems trimmed, quartered
     Salt and freshly ground black pepper
1½   pounds (750 g) green beans, trimmed and cut into short lengths
6   tablespoons all-purpose (plain) flour
2   cups (500 ml) milk
1   pinch cayenne pepper
1   pinch grated nutmeg
1   cup (120 g) freshly grated Parmesan cheese
¼   cup (30 g) fine dry bread crumbs
¼   cup (60 ml) extra-virgin olive oil
4   shallots, cut crosswise into thin rings

Serves 4–6 • Preparation 30 minutes • Cooking 40–45 minutes Difficulty 1

1. Preheat the oven to 375°F (190°C/gas 5). Melt 2 tablespoons of butter in a large frying pan over medium heat. Add the onion and saute until softened, 3–4 minutes. Add the bell pepper and mushrooms and cook until softened, 8–10 minutes. Season with 1 teaspoon of salt and ¼ teaspoon pepper. Set aside to cool.

2. Bring a saucepan of water to a boil. Add the beans, and cook until just tender, 4–5 minutes. Drain and let cool a little. Toss with the mushroom mixture and set aside.

3. Melt the remaining 4 tablespoons of butter in a medium saucepan over medium heat. Add 4 tablespoons of flour, whisk constantly until mixture begins to turn golden. Pour in milk and whisk until thickened, 3–4 minutes. Stir in the cayenne, and nutmeg, and season with salt and pepper. Pour over beans, and toss to combine.

4. Butter a 9 x13-inch (23 x 30-cm) baking dish. Spread half the green bean mixture over the bottom. Sprinkle with half the Parmesan, and top with the remaining beans. Sprinkle with the remaining Parmesan and the bread crumbs. Cover with aluminum foil.

5. Heat the oil in a small frying pan over medium-high heat. Toss the shallots with the remaining 2 tablespoons of flour, and fry until golden brown.

6. Bake for 15–20 minutes, until bubbling and golden brown. Sprinkle with the fried shallots, and serve hot.

You can prepare this dish ahead of time and chill in the refrigerator until ready to bake.

CAULIFLOWER gratin

¼	cup (60 g) unsalted butter
2	heads Belgian endive, cut lengthwise into sixths
1	cup (150 g) Israeli (large grain) couscous
2	large heads cauliflower, cut into florets
¼	cup all-purpose flour
3	cups (750 g) milk
2	tablespoons finely chopped fresh marjoram
1	teaspoon salt
¼	teaspoon freshly ground black pepper
¼	teaspoon nutmeg
⅛	teaspoon cayenne pepper
3	cups (350 g) freshly grated Gruyère cheese
¼	cup fresh bread crumbs
⅓	cup (50 g) coarsely grated Parmesan cheese

Serves 6–8 • Preparation 15 minutes • Cooking 1¼ hours • Difficulty 1

1. Preheat the oven to 400°F (200°C/gas 6). Butter a 6-cup (1.5-liter) ovenproof dish. Put the endive in the dish. Top with the couscous and cover with the cauliflower.

2. Melt the butter in a saucepan over medium heat. Whisk in the flour. Reduce the heat to low and stir for 2 minutes. Whisk in the milk and simmer, stirring constantly, until thickened. Remove from the heat. Stir in the marjoram, salt, pepper, nutmeg, cayenne, and cheese until smooth. Pour over the cauliflower. Sprinkle with bread crumbs.

3. Bake for 30 minutes. Sprinkle with the Parmesan. Reduce the oven temperature to 350°F (180°C/gas 4) and bake until tender, about 40 minutes. Serve hot.

EGGPLANT parmigiana

2   large eggs
³/₄   cup (120 g) fine dry bread
        crumbs
³/₄   cup (100 g) finely grated
        Parmesan cheese + 4
        tablespoons for topping
1   teaspoon dried oregano
¹/₂   teaspoon dried basil
        Salt and ground pepper
2   large eggplants, peeled and
        sliced into ¹/₂-inch (1-cm) thick
        rounds
6   cups (1.5 liters) store-bought
        chunky tomato sauce
12   ounces (350 g) shredded
        mozzarella cheese

Serves 4–6 • Preparation 45 minutes • Cooking 1¹/₂ hours • Difficulty 2

1. Preheat the oven to 375°F (190°C/gas 5). Brush two baking sheets with oil. Beat the eggs and 2 tablespoons of water in a bowl. Combine the bread crumbs, ³/₄ cup of Parmesan, oregano, basil, salt, and pepper in another bowl.

2. Dip the eggplant in the egg mixture, and dredge in the bread crumb mixture, coating well. Place on the baking sheets. Bake for 20–25 minutes, until golden brown. Turn and bake for 20–25 minutes more. Remove from the oven. Increase the oven temperature to 400°F (200°C/gas 6).

3. Spread 2 cups of sauce in a 9 x 13-inch (23 x 33-cm) baking dish. Arrange half the eggplant in the dish. Cover with 2 cups of sauce, then some mozzarella. Repeat, finishing with Parmesan.

4. Bake for 20–25 minutes, until bubbling and golden. Let stand for 5 minutes before serving.

just desserts

RASPBERRY tart

Crust

1¹/₃	cups (200 g) all-purpose (plain) flour
¹/₂	cup (120 ml) cold unsalted butter, cut into small pieces
¹/₃	cup (70 g) sugar
¹/₄	teaspoon salt
	Fresh cream, to serve (optional)

Filling

8	ounces (250 g) cream cheese, softened
¹/₄	cup (50 g) sugar
5	cups (750 g) fresh raspberries
¹/₄	cup (75 g) seedless red currant jelly

Serves 6 • Preparation 30 minutes + 2–7 hours to set & chill • Cooking 25–30 minutes • Difficulty 2

Crust

1. Preheat the oven to 350°F (180°C/gas 4). Pulse the flour, butter, sugar, and salt in a food processor until moist crumbs form.

2. Transfer the dough to a 9-inch (23-cm) tart pan with a removable bottom. Press evenly into the bottom and up the sides of the pan. Chill until firm, about 30 minutes.

3. Prick all over with a fork. Bake for 25–30 minutes, until golden. Let cool completely in the pan.

Filling

1. Beat the cream cheese and sugar in a bowl until smooth. Spread evenly over the baked crust. Arrange the berries in tight concentric circles over the cream cheese.

2. Heat the jelly over low heat until liquid. Brush over the berries. Let set for 30 minutes. Chill in the pan for 1–6 hours. Slice and serve with fresh cream, if liked.

If you liked this recipe, you will love these as well.

PURPLE FRUIT salad

CHOCOLATE-DIPPED
almond strawberries

STRAWBERRY CREAM
cake

PURPLE FRUIT salad

3	tablespoons light brown sugar
1/4	cup (60 ml) freshly squeezed lime juice
3	purple plums, halved, pitted, and cut into small pieces
2	cups (300 g) seedless red grapes
1	cup (150 g) blackberries
1	cup (150 g) blueberries
	Greek yogurt, to serve.

Serves 4–6 • Preparation 15 minutes + 2 hours to chill • Difficulty 1

1. Whisk the brown sugar and lime juice in a small bowl until the sugar is dissolved.

2. Put the plums, grapes, blackberries, and blueberries in a bowl and toss to combine. Chill for at least 2 hours.

3. Spoon into serving glasses. Garnish each one with a dollop of yogurt, and serve.

CHOCOLATE-DIPPED almond strawberries

8 ounces (250 g) dark chocolate, finely chopped

1 pound (500 g) large strawberries, green stalks attached

1/3 cup (70 g) finely chopped almonds

Serves 6 • Preparation 15 minutes + 15 minutes to set • Cooking 5 minutes • Difficulty 1

1. Melt the chocolate in a double boiler over barely simmering water, or in the microwave. Remove from the heat. Line a baking sheet with parchment paper.

2. Dip each strawberry into the chocolate, twirling to coat. Sprinkle the chocolate with almonds, and place on the prepared baking sheet.

3. Chill the strawberries until the chocolate is set, at least 15 minutes, before serving.

FREE FORM APPLE pie

2	cups (300 g) all-purpose (plain) flour
$1/2$	cup (75 g) whole-wheat (wholemeal) flour
1	cup (250 g) cold unsalted butter, cut into pieces
5	tablespoons sugar
1	teaspoon salt
$1/2$	cup (120 ml) iced water
$1/4$	cup (40 g) whole, skin-on almonds, toasted
2	tablespoons cornstarch (cornflour)
1	teaspoon ground cinnamon
3	baking apples halved, cored, and thinly sliced (keep slices together)
2	tablespoons freshly squeezed lemon juice
4	tablespoons raw sugar
	Vanilla ice cream, to serve

Serves 6–8 • Preparation 20 minutes + 1$1/2$ hours to chill • Cooking 45–50 minutes • Difficulty 2

1. Combine both flours, the butter, 1 tablespoon of sugar, and the salt in a food processor. Pulse until the mixture resembles fine crumbs. Sprinkle with half the iced water. Pulse until the dough is crumbly but still holds together when squeezed. If it is too dry, add extra ice water, 1 tablespoon at a time. Shape the dough into a disk, wrap in plastic wrap (cling film), and chill for 1 hour.

2. Combine the almonds, remaining 4 tablespoons of sugar, the cornstarch, and cinnamon in a food processor. Pulse until ground to a coarse meal.

3. Line a large baking sheet with parchment paper.

4. Roll out the dough on a lightly floured work surface to $1/4$-inch (5-mm) thick. Transfer to the prepared baking sheet. Sprinkle the almond mixture over the dough.

5. Arrange the apples on the dough. Leave a 2-inch (5-cm) border all around the edges. Fold the edges of the dough over the fruit. Drizzle with the lemon juice and sprinkle with the raw sugar. Chill for 30 minutes.

6. Preheat the oven to 350°F (180°C/gas 4). Bake until the crust is golden brown and the apples are tender, 45–50 minutes. Serve hot, with a scoop or two of ice cream on each serving.

RHUBARB crumble

Rhubarb

1³/₄ pounds (800 g) rhubarb, trimmed, cut into short pieces

1 cup (200 g) sugar

2 tablespoons cornstarch (cornflour)

¹/₄ teaspoon salt

Crumble

1 cup (150 g) all-purpose (plain) flour

¹/₂ cup (100 g) firmly packed light brown sugar

3 tablespoons sugar

¹/₄ teaspoon salt

¹/₂ cup (120 g) cold unsalted butter, cut into small pieces

Fresh cream or ice cream, to serve

Serves 4–6 • Preparation 30 minutes + 15 minutes to chill • Cooking 1¹/₂ hours • Difficulty 1

Rhubarb

1. Set out a 9-inch (23-cm) pie plate. Preheat the oven to 400°F (200°C/gas 6).

2. Toss the rhubarb with the sugar, cornstarch, and salt in a bowl. Pour into the pie plate.

Crumble

1. Combine the flour, both sugars, and salt in a bowl. Rub in the butter until large, moist clumps form. Chill for 15 minutes. Sprinkle over the rhubarb in the pie plate.

2. Reduce the oven temperature to 350°F (180°C/gas 4). Bake until the topping is golden brown, about 1¹/₂ hours. Serve hot with fresh cream or ice cream.

BLACKBERRY cobbler

Filling

1½	pounds (750 g) blackberries
¾	cup (150 g) sugar
2	tablespoons cornstarch (cornflour)
¼	teaspoon salt

Topping

2	cups (300 g) all-purpose (plain) flour
2	teaspoons baking powder
⅓	cup (70 g) brown sugar
¼	teaspoon salt
½	cup (120 g) cold unsalted butter
1	cup (250 ml) heavy (double) cream
	Raw sugar, to sprinkle

Serves 6–8 • Preparation 15 minutes + 30 minutes to cool • Cooking 1 hour • Difficulty 1

Filling

1. Preheat the oven to 375°F (190°C/gas 5). Combine the blackberries, sugar, cornstarch, and salt in a 9 x 12-inch (23 x 30-cm) baking dish.

Topping

1. Combine the flour, baking powder, brown sugar, and salt in a bowl. Rub in the butter until the largest pieces are the size of small peas. Add the cream (you may not need it all), and use a fork to incorporate, stirring until absorbed.

2. Turn out the dough onto a clean work surface, and knead briefly. Press into a ball then pat to about 1 inch (2.5 cm) thick. Cut into eight rectangles, and place over the filling. Brush with cream, and sprinkle with the raw sugar.

3. Bake for about 1 hour, until golden brown and cooked through. Let stand for 30 minutes. Serve warm, with the remaining cream.

PINE NUT cookies

Makes 30–35 cookies • Preparation 15 minutes • Cooking 15–20 minutes • Difficulty 1

2	cups (240 g) pine nuts	1	large egg
1	cup (150 g) confectioners' (icing) sugar	1/2	cup (75 g) all-purpose (plain) flour
1/4	cup almond paste	1/4	teaspoon baking powder
1	teaspoon vanilla extract (essence)	1/4	teaspoon salt

1. Preheat the oven to 350°F (180°C/gas 4). Line two large baking sheets with parchment paper.
2. Chop 1 cup (120 g) of the pine nuts, the sugar, almond paste, and vanilla in a food processor until fine crumbs form. Add the egg and pulse to combine. Add the flour, baking powder, and salt and pulse until the dough comes together.
3. Roll the dough into walnut-size balls. Roll the balls in the remaining pine nuts, gently pressing to coat. Place on the prepared baking sheets, spacing 1 inch (2.5 cm) apart.
4. Bake for 15–20 minutes, until golden brown. Let cool completely on the baking sheets on wire racks.

CARROT muffins

Makes 12 muffins • Preparation 20 minutes • Cooking 20 minutes • Difficulty 1

Muffins

2	cups (300 g) all-purpose (plain) flour	1 1/2	cups (200 g) finely grated carrots
1/2	cup (75 g) whole-wheat (wholemeal) flour	1/2	cup (120 ml) milk
1	tablespoon baking powder	1/4	cup (60 ml) freshly squeezed lemon juice
3/4	cup (150 g) firmly packed brown sugar		**Lemon Frosting**
1/2	cup (120 g) salted butter, melted	8	ounces (250 g) cream cheese, softened
2	large eggs, beaten	1	cup (150 g) confectioners' (icing) sugar
		1	tablespoon finely grated unwaxed lemon zest

Muffins

1. Preheat the oven to 350°F (180°C/gas 4). Line a 12-cup muffin pan with paper liners. Combine both flours, the baking powder, and sugar in a bowl. Stir in the butter, eggs, carrots, milk, and lemon juice. Spoon into the muffin cups. Bake for 20–25 minutes, until golden. Cool completely on wire racks.

Lemon Frosting

1. Beat the cream cheese, confectioners' sugar, and lemon zest in a bowl until creamy. Spread on the muffins.

RASPBERRY muffins

Makes 12 muffins • Preparation 15 minutes • Cooking 15–20 minutes • Difficulty 1

1	cup (150 g) all-purpose (plain) flour		packed light brown sugar
1 1/2	teaspoons baking powder	1	large egg
1/2	teaspoon baking soda (bicarbonate of soda)	2	tablespoons sunflower oil
1	teaspoon ground cinnamon	1	teaspoon vanilla extract (essence)
2/3	cup (150 g) low-fat plain yogurt	1	cup (150 g) fresh raspberries
1/2	cup (100 g) firmly	4	tablespoons raw sugar

1. Preheat the oven to 400°F (200°C/gas 6). Line a 12-cup muffin pan with paper liners.
2. Combine the flour, baking powder, baking soda, and cinnamon in a bowl. Whisk the yogurt, brown sugar, egg, sunflower oil, and vanilla in another bowl. Pour the yogurt mixture into the flour mixture and stir until just combined. Stir in the raspberries.
3. Spoon the batter into the muffin cups. Sprinkle each muffin with some raw sugar. Bake for 15–20 minutes, until risen and springy to the touch. Turn out onto wire racks. Serve warm.

FRUIT & NUT cookies

Makes 40–50 cookies • Preparation 30 minutes • Cooking 12–15 minutes • Difficulty 2

2 1/4	cups (330 g) all-purpose (plain) flour	1	teaspoon vanilla extract
1	teaspoon baking soda (bicarbonate of soda)	1 1/2	cups (150 g) shredded (dessicated) coconut
1	teaspoon salt	1 1/2	cups (120 g) chopped dried apricots
1	cup (250 g) butter	1 1/2	cups (120 g) chopped dates
1	cup (200 g) firmly packed dark brown sugar	1 1/2	cups (180 g) chopped pecans
1/2	cup (100 g) sugar	1 1/2	cups (180 g) chopped pistachios
2	large eggs		

1. Preheat the oven to 350°F (180°C/gas 4). Line three large baking sheets with parchment paper. Sift the flour, baking soda, and salt into a bowl.
2. Beat the butter and both sugars until creamy. Beat in the eggs one at a time. Add the vanilla. Beat in the flour mixture until just combined. Stir in the coconut, apricots, dates, pecans, and pistachios.
3. Drop 2 heaped tablespoons of dough at a time onto the prepared baking sheets, spacing 2 inches (5 cm) apart. Flatten slightly.
4. Bake for 12–15 minutes, until golden brown. Let cool completely on the baking sheets on wire racks.

SPECIAL OCCASION carrot cake

Cake

2¹/₂ cups (375 g) all-purpose (plain) flour

1 teaspoon baking powder

1 teaspoon baking soda (bicarbonate of soda)

1 teaspoon ground cinnamon

¹/₂ teaspoon salt

¹/₂ teaspoon ground ginger

¹/₄ teaspoon ground nutmeg

1¹/₂ cups (370 g) unsalted butter, softened

1 cup (200 g) firmly packed light brown sugar

¹/₂ cup (100 g) sugar

3 large eggs

2 teaspoons vanilla extract (essence)

¹/₂ cup (120 ml) water

1 pound (500 g) carrots, peeled and finely shredded (about 2³/₄ cups)

1 cup (120 g) pecans, finely chopped

1 cup (120 g) pumpkin seeds

Cream Cheese Frosting

1 pound (500 g) cream cheese, softened

2 teaspoons vanilla extract (essence)

1 cup (250 g) unsalted butter, cut into pieces, softened

2 pounds (1 kg) confectioners' sugar

Serves 10–12 • Preparation 45 minutes + 1 hour to chill • Cooking 30 minutes • Difficulty 2

Cake

1. Preheat the oven to 350°F (180°C/gas 4). Butter three 9-inch (23-cm) round cake pans. Line the bottoms with parchment paper. Sift the flour, baking powder, baking soda, cinnamon, salt, ginger, and nutmeg into a bowl.

2. Beat the butter and both sugars in a bowl until creamy. Add the eggs one at a time, beating until just combined after each addition. Add the vanilla, water, and carrots, beating until combined. Gradually beat in the flour mixture, followed by the chopped pecans.

3. Spoon the batter evenly into the prepared pans. Bake for about 30 minutes, until golden brown and a toothpick inserted into the centers comes out clean. Let cool in the pans on a wire rack for 15 minutes. Run a knife around the edges of the pans to loosen, and turn out onto a wire rack. Let cool completely.

Cream Cheese Frosting

1. Beat the cream cheese, vanilla, and butter until pale and creamy. Gradually add the confectioners' sugar, beating until smooth and well combined.

2. Trim the rounded tops off two of the cakes. Place one trimmed cake on a serving platter. Spread with 1 cup of the frosting. Top with the second trimmed cake and spread with 1 cup of frosting. Top with the remaining domed cake. Spread the remaining frosting over the top and sides of the cake. Gently press the pumpkin seeds into the sides of the cake. Chill for 1 hour before serving.

MAPLE & PECAN squares

Base

1¼   cups (180 g) all-purpose
      (plain) flour
½   teaspoon salt
¼   cup (40 g) coarsely chopped
      toasted pecans
½   cup (120 g) + unsalted butter,
      softened
¼   cup (50 g) firmly packed light
      brown sugar
1   tablespoon maple syrup

Topping

⅓   cup (90 g) unsalted butter,
      softened
½   cup (80 g) coarsely chopped
      toasted pecans
¼   teaspoon salt
3   tablespoons light brown sugar
1   tablespoon maple syrup
¼   cup finely chopped candied
      (glacé) ginger
¼   cup (50 g) sugar
2   tablespoons light corn
      (golden) syrup
3   tablespoons heavy (double)
      cream

Serves 4–6 • Preparation 30 minutes + 30 minutes to chill • Cooking 20–25 minutes • Difficulty 2

Base

1. Butter an 8-inch (20-cm) square baking pan. Line with parchment paper, leaving a 2-inch (5-cm) overhang on two sides. Preheat the oven to 350°F (180°C/gas 4).

2. Stir the flour, salt, and nuts in a bowl. Beat the butter and brown sugar until creamy. Mix in the flour mixture and maple syrup. Press the dough evenly into the prepared pan. Chill for 30 minutes.

3. Bake for 20–25 minutes, until pale golden brown. Transfer to a wire rack and let cool slightly.

Topping

1. Put the butter and pecans in a small saucepan. Stir constantly over medium-high heat for 2–3 minutes. Add the salt, brown sugar, maple syrup, ginger, sugar, corn syrup, and cream. Boil, stirring constantly, for 2 minutes. Spread over the base.

2. Let cool completely. Lift out of the pan using the overhanging paper. Cut into squares and serve.

DRIED FRUIT & NUT bars

8	ounces (250 g) pitted dates
1½	cups (200 g) old-fashioned oats, finely ground
1	cup (150 g) pecans, toasted, half finely ground and half coarsely chopped
½	cup (60 g) unsalted macadamia nuts, toasted, half finely ground and half coarsely chopped
⅓	cup (60 g) dried mango, chopped
⅓	cup (60 g) dried cherries, chopped
⅓	cup (60 g) dried blueberries
2	tablespoons oat bran
3	tablespoons ground flaxseed
2	tablespoons wheat germ
½	teaspoon salt
½	teaspoon ground cinnamon
3	tablespoons honey

Serves 8 • Preparation 20 minutes • Cooking 20–25 minutes • Difficulty 1

1. Preheat the oven to 350°F (180°C/gas 4). Oil an 8-inch (20-cm) square baking pan.

2. Place the dates in a small saucepan, cover with cold water, and bring to a boil. Drain well, then chop in a food processor until smooth.

3. Mix the oats, pecans, macadamias, mango, cherries, blueberries, bran, flaxseed, wheat germ, salt, and cinnamon in a bowl. Stir in the date purée and honey. Press into the pan in an even layer.

4. Bake for 20–25 minutes, until golden. Let cool completely in the pan on a wire rack. Cut into eight bars and serve.

Serve this luscious cream cake on special occasions. You could easily replace the strawberries with raspberries, sliced peaches, kiwi fruit, or other fresh fruit of your choice.

STRAWBERRY CREAM cake

Cake

1¹/₂	cups (225 g) all-purpose (plain) flour
2	teaspoons baking powder
¹/₂	teaspoon salt
¹/₂	cup (120 g) unsalted butter, softened
¹/₂	cup (100 g) sugar
2	large eggs + 2 large egg yolks
¹/₂	teaspoon vanilla extract (essence)
¹/₂	cup (120 ml) milk

Topping

1	pound (500 g) strawberries, thinly sliced
¹/₂	cup (100 g) sugar
2	tablespoons cold water
1	teaspoon unflavored gelatin
1¹/₂	cups (375 ml) heavy (double) cream

Serves 8–10 • Preparation 30 minutes • Cooking 30–35 minutes Difficulty 2

Cake

1. Preheat the oven to 350°F (180°C/gas 4). Butter an 8-inch (20-cm) round cake pan and line with parchment paper. Sift the flour, baking powder, and salt into a bowl.

2. Beat the butter and sugar in a bowl until pale and creamy. Add the eggs and egg yolks one at a time, beating until just combined after each addition. Add the vanilla. Gradually beat in the flour mixture, alternating with the milk. Spoon the batter into the prepared pan.

3. Bake for 30–35 minutes, until a toothpick inserted into the center comes out clean. Cool in the pan for 10 minutes, then turn out onto a wire rack and let cool completely. Using a serrated knife, split the cake in half horizontally. Put the bottom half, cut-side up, on a serving plate.

Topping

1. Combine the strawberries and ¹/₄ cup (50 g) of sugar in a bowl. Place the water in a small saucepan and sprinkle with the gelatin. Let soften for 5 minutes. Place the saucepan over very low heat and stir until the gelatin is dissolved. Remove from the heat and let cool.

2. Beat the cream and remaining ¹/₄ cup (50 g) of sugar in a bowl until soft peaks form. Continue beating while gradually adding the gelatin mixture. Beat until thickened.

3. Spread half the cream mixture over the bottom cake layer. Top with half the strawberries. Cover with the remaining cake layer. Top with the remaining cream mixture and strawberries. Chill until ready to serve.

INDEX